Beneath Cornish Seas

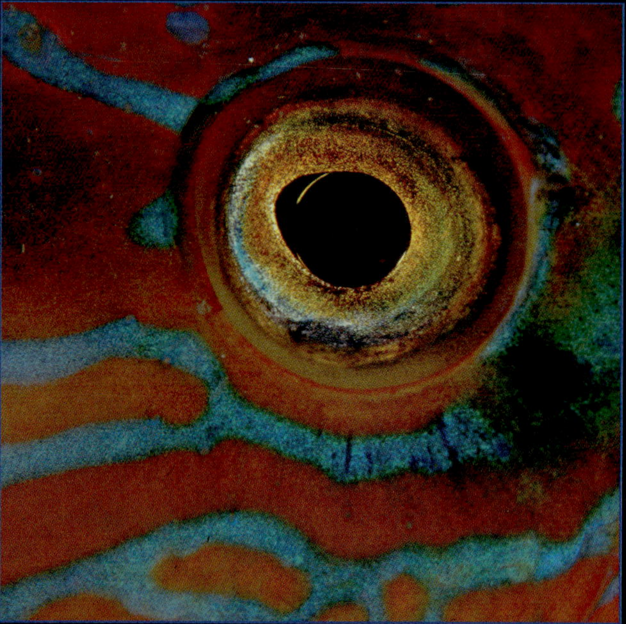

MARK WEBSTER

First published in 2009 by
Alison Hodge, 2 Clarence Place, Penzance, Cornwall TR18 2QA, UK
www.alison-hodge.co.uk info@alison-hodge.co.uk

www.photec.co.uk markwebster@photec.co.uk

ISBN-13 978-0-906720-70-7

British Library Cataloguing-in-Publication Data
A catalogue record for this book is available from the British Library.

Designed and originated by BDP –
Book Development & Production, Penzance, Cornwall

Cover design: Christopher Laughton

Printed in China on paper produced with elemental chlorine-free pulp, harvested from managed sustainable forests.

A Darwin 200 celebration

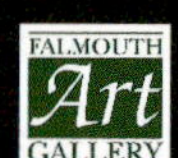

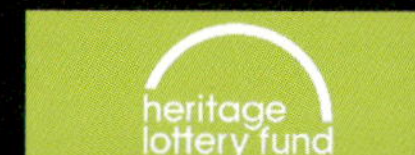

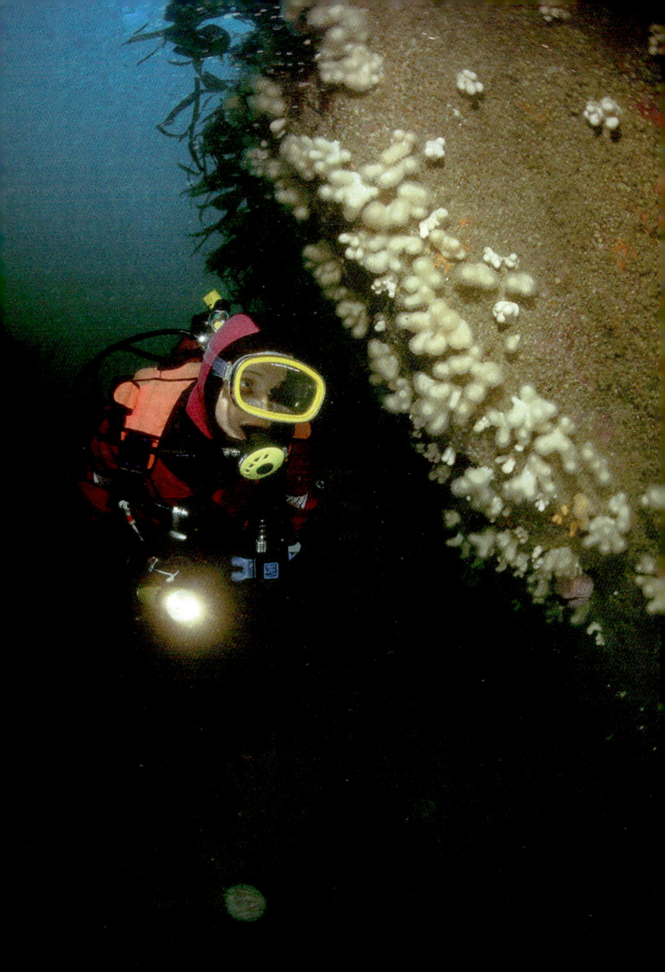

Introduction

Cornwall is physically remote from the remainder of the British Isles, with a mild climate and miles of unspoiled coast and secluded beaches. The rugged granite of the peninsula juts out into the Atlantic, creating a stark contrast between the calm inlets, coves and fishing villages of the south coast and the dramatic, towering cliffs and the might of the open ocean on the north coast. The hard rock extends hidden far out to sea, forming reefs and pinnacles, which teem with life.

The popular image of calm blue seas in summer, and dark grey or green cold water pounding the coast during relentless winter storms is only half the story. Hidden below the surface of these temperate waters is a rich array of colourful marine life, with a diversity that can challenge a tropical reef; indeed many of our own species are closely related to those in warm waters.

The Gulf Stream divides around the peninsula on its path north, and the warmer, clearer waters it carries support a diversity of indigenous and visiting marine life not generally found elsewhere around the UK's coastline. The headlands and offshore reefs are bombarded by nutrients borne by the strong tides, which feed a multitude of invertebrate species, including anemones, soft and stony corals, and even sea fans more commonly found on coral reefs. These organisms appear to paint the rocks with carpets of colour, giving an almost tropical feel to many reefs. Fish life is profuse, with shoals of bass and mackerel, reef-dwelling wrasse, flatfish, blennies, scorpion fish, tope, sharks, and a variety of occasional visitors from warmer, southern waters. During warm summers we can expect to see trigger fish, sun fish and even leatherback turtles. Large species like the basking shark are common in early summer, and in recent years the numbers sited have run into the hundreds. The variety is almost endless. Hopefully this book will give you an insight into the life to be found in our rock pools and just below the waves.

Geology

Cornwall's spectacular landscape and coastline is largely due to the varied geology of the peninsula. There is a mixture of sedimentary rocks, laid down during periods of high sea levels, overlaying rock intrusions of volcanic or igneous origin. In many places the granite just peaks through at high points in the form of 'tors' or caps of hard rock. But at Land's End and for large stretches of the north coast, the granite is dominant, forming an impressive coastline with plunging cliffs dissected by sweeping beaches of fine granite sand. On the Lizard, the most southerly point of the UK, there is yet another variation of the intrusion in the serpentine cliffs, thrust up through the ocean floor to expose rocks not normally seen, from an area deep below the earth's crust, that lies some 10 km (6 ml) below the surface.

Geological activity, and the changes and movements associated with freezing and thawing during the ice age, has created the diversity that makes Cornwall so fascinating and attractive.

Habitat variety

The varied geology has led to different kinds of marine habitats around the Cornish coast, each with unique features. On the south coast are the lush river valleys of the Helford, the Fowey and the Fal, the latter of which forms the third largest natural deep-water anchorage in the world. The tidal estuaries of these rivers are rich in marine life, and often teem with juvenile fish.

These river systems were 'drowned' at the end of the last ice age, by a combination of sinking land and rising sea levels. The Fal in particular offers quite dramatic profiles under water, from shallow, drowned flood plains to the remnants of the original river valley which penetrates far inland, retaining depths of up to 35 m (110 ft). The industrial revolution and expansion of the nineteenth and early twentieth centuries threatened these habitats with careless waste disposal from copper and tin mining and china clay extraction. Fortunately recent decades have propagated a more educated and enlightened appreciation of the damage caused by pollution, and now strict controls and marine reserves have returned many areas to their former glory.

In the shallow waters of these rivers are the most northern concentrations of eel grass, common in the Mediterranean, and an attractive breeding ground for all manner of marine life. In the spring, clusters of eggs are to be found at the base of the eel grass stalks, deposited by fish, nudibranchs (sea slugs), squid and cuttlefish. Where the water is a little deeper, there are sweeping beds of maerl – a form of calcified algae that forms little coral-like clusters. The fauna of the maerl beds is very rich, with many species of fish, crustaceans, worms and molluscs hiding among the delicate branches. A little further up the Fal estuary are thriving beds of wild oysters, which can only be fished commercially by hand from licensed punts.

Rock pools

For many of us, our first experience of marine life is on a rocky foreshore, exploring rock pools exposed at low tide. These miniature aquariums may seem lifeless at first, but a little patient observation soon reveals them to be brimming with small inhabitants. The fascination created by these marine microcosms never pales, and we can learn an enormous amount by following the tide out and dipping into the rock pools as they are revealed.

Rock pools come in a variety of sizes: some are ankle deep and easily negotiated with a stride; others are big enough to swim or snorkel in. The creatures within them vary from those that specialize in an inter-tidal existence to those that are stranded temporarily until the next high water allows them to escape. Barnacles, limpets, top shells, anemones, hydroids, starfish and numerous other sessile species colonize the rock surfaces, often covered or disguised by floating seaweed. Carefully parting the weed will reveal these treasures, and also expose the habitat at the bottom of the pool. Here there may be sand or gravel and numerous small stones and rocks that provide shelter for blennies, shannies, butterfish, pipefish, prawns, shrimps, and several species of crab. Other species hide in different ways, using camouflage or a borrowed mobile home for shelter. Scorpion fish, dabs and invertebrates such as sea hares use camouflage for protection or predation, while the hermit crab protects its soft body by borrowing a discarded top shell or winkle shell.

All these species continue their lives within the protection of the pool until the tide surges back to cover them. Life can be precarious here in the inter-tidal zone, particularly when the weather is stormy, and many mature species retreat to deeper waters just offshore for protection in the winter months. So the best time to explore rock pools is in spring and summer, when the sea is calmer and new and juvenile life is thriving and using the isolation between tides to protect itself from predators. Approach the pools carefully, and avoid casting a shadow which will alert nervous residents to your presence. Bring a small net and bucket, and perhaps a magnifying glass to examine your catch; but be sure to treat all your finds gently, and return them

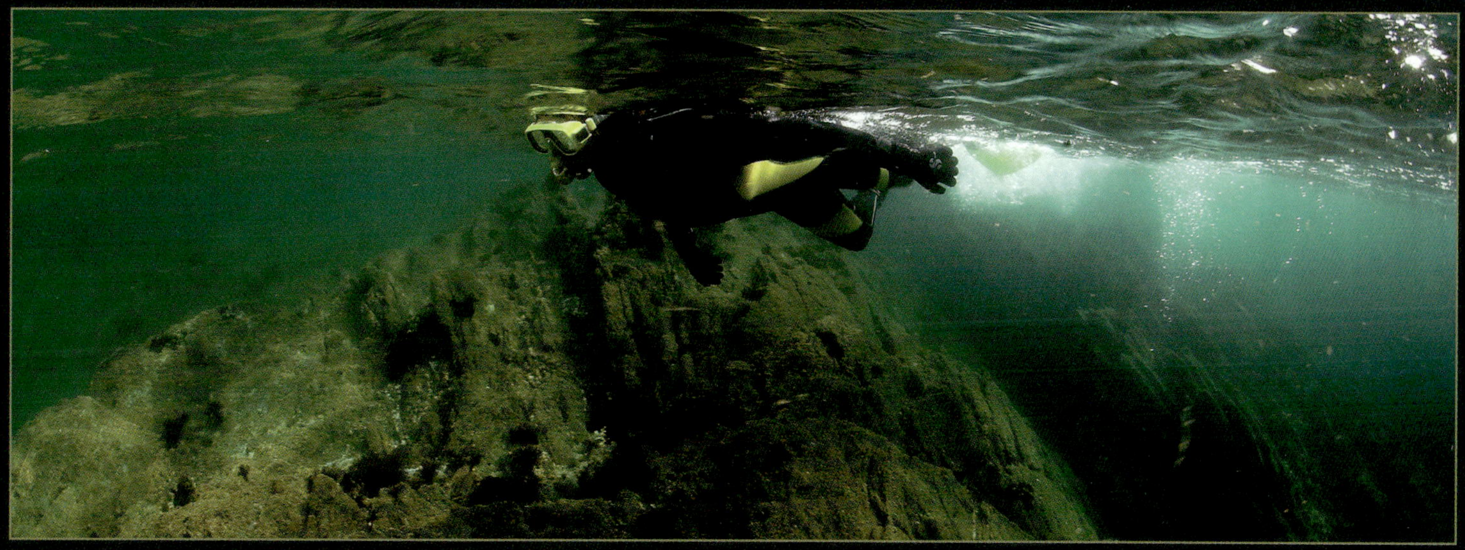

Snorkeller explores the fringing reef at Pendennis Point, Falmouth

to the pool which they are using as home. Slow movements and patience will be rewarded with some fascinating discoveries.

Inshore reefs

The coastal topography varies dramatically from sheltered bays and coves to sheer cliffs that plunge straight into the sea. They have in common the same rich marine life that inhabits both the littoral zone and the shallow reefs, gullies and caves. During the winter months these inshore areas are often lashed by severe storms swept in from the Atlantic, but as spring arrives the waters become calmer, and the annual cycle of life commences once more. In summer the shallows are full of beds of bootlace and lettuce seaweeds, which offer protection to juveniles and so are a favourite hunting ground for small shoals of large grey mullet that prey on the newly hatched fish and plankton.

As with many other temperate sea areas, there are kelp seaweed forests that dominate the shallow waters and reef tops inshore. The kelp here does not reach the proportions of the giant species of the Californian coast, but it is equally prolific and provides a wide range of habitats among its fronds, stypes and holdfasts. The depth to which it extends varies with topography and water clarity. Generally it clings to the top of the rocks and gullies to a depth of 10 m (33 ft), whereas on deeper reefs further offshore, where waters are clearer, kelp can be found growing as deep as 20 m (66 ft).

The reefs are often dissected by deep cuts and gullies, all crying out to be explored, with steps and ledges leading you towards the surface. Even in the shallows, where many rock faces are exposed to tidal current, filter-feeding species like the soft coral *Alcyonium digitatum* (known locally as dead men's fingers), jewel anemones and sponges all thrive.

The fish life on these shallow reefs includes several varieties of wrasse, the largest being the ballan wrasse, which is our equivalent of the coral trout or grouper. Ballan wrasse are very territorial. The large males can reach lengths of 60 cm (2 ft) or more and come in a variety of colours, including a striking deep red speckled pattern. The females can grow almost as large, but tend to be slightly duller in colouration, ranging from green to brown. In the springtime you will often see them in pairs, with the female carrying a heavy brood of eggs which the male is anxious to fertilize during spawning. These fish are very inquisitive, and will often make repeated approaches through the kelp if you are patient enough to stay in one spot for a few minutes. Look out also for feeding activity on the reef edge in the sand and gravel, where you will also often see them rubbing their bodies on the seabed, apparently to remove parasites. You might be lucky enough to observe another species of wrasse, the goldsinney, actually removing parasites from the larger fish, just like a cleaning station on a tropical reef.

Two other very colourful species of wrasse are common on shallow reefs. The male cuckoo wrasse is resplendent in snazzy blue and orange livery, and can be very persistent in his approaches when you enter his territory. He may become aggressive, particularly when he sees his reflection in a camera port, and the males have been known to nip at exposed skin, which can come as quite a shock when you have your eye glued to the viewfinder! The female cuckoo wrasse is much duller to look at, sporting a drab brownish livery. However, when a male dies or departs a territory, the most dominant female begins a transition to become a male, and you may encounter an odd-looking fish that is only half way through the change of life. The other colourful resident wrasse is the male corkwing, which has an intricate swirling pattern of blue, red and brown, and is most likely to be seen in spring building a nest among the kelp, in

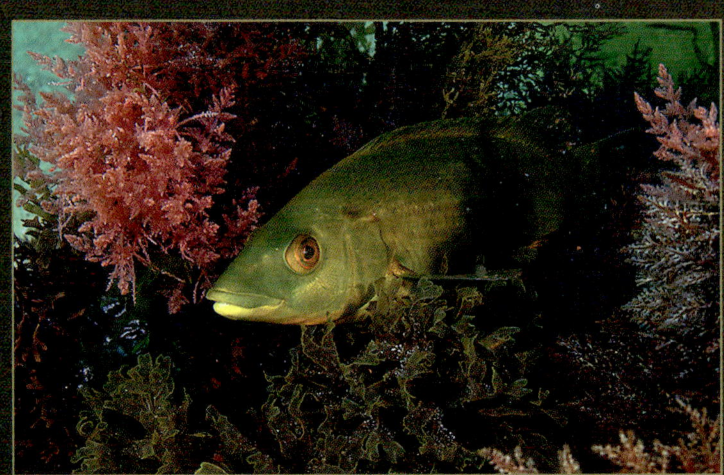

Ballan wrasse among multi-coloured seaweeds

preparation for the female to spawn. If you spot one, try to track his movements across the reef and you will soon be led to the nest site, which will give you the opportunity to get closer still.

Other kelp-hunters include the pollack, which hangs above the weed or close to the sand, often in small groups, much like a barracuda waiting to strike. More difficult to spot are the strange-looking John Dory, whose bodies are wafer-thin when viewed head-on – a feature which, coupled with flawless colouration, helps them blend perfectly into the kelp and seaweeds. However, they will often track you in the hope that you will disturb something worth eating. If you are fortunate, you might see one strike in a flash, with its amazing extending jaw, which sucks the prey back in towards the fish's mouth.

Almost every reef has numerous inhabitants which may not be obvious at first glance, but which, with a little patience, you will begin to track down. Many of the fish you will find in the cracks and crevices of the reef are territorial or semi-sessile, and are easily approached for a closer look. The smiling features of the tompot blenny are almost irresistible, but there are also Montagu's and Yarrel's blenny, shannies and butterfish to be found. A number of gobies share the reef habitat with the blennies, the most striking being leopard-spotted gobies, generally found in small sandy openings at the base of the reef. Less obvious species include scorpion fish and topknot flatfish, both of which have excellent camouflage and are more challenging to hunt down, but usually equally co-operative once found. In late spring and early summer you will find many species of fish tending their egg clusters. These are normally the males, guarding the nursery for perhaps three to four weeks. They include butterfish, shannies, tompot blennies, corkwing wrasse and the weird-looking lumpsucker, which normally dwells in deep water for the rest of the year.

On the sand

Wherever we explore, the temptation is to focus on the reef, which usually offers the greatest concentration of sea life. You might ignore the sandy areas bordering a reef, or the often large areas of sand and gravel between the reef outcrops, in the belief that they are barren areas devoid of interesting life. However, these apparent deserts are surprisingly well populated, particularly in the shallow waters in early spring, when formerly lifeless areas begin to sprout new growths of seaweed, stands of bootlace weeds and eel grass peppered with anemones and tube worms. These in turn are populated by fry and juveniles, which attract predators. The weedy areas are a great place to spot species like sticklebacks and pipefish, which blend easily as they hang motionless or move slowly through this natural camouflage. There are two species common in our waters – the greater pipefish, which has a head very much like a seahorse and an armoured appearance to its body, and the snake pipefish, which is altogether smoother and more colourful, and is often found with a series of pale bands down the length of its body. Seahorses are apparently making a comeback, and there are increasing reports of sightings and capture of these critters in crab pots all along the south coast. They also favour the weed on the sandy areas, but are small and incredibly well camouflaged, so you will need a great deal of patience and a good chunk of luck to spot one.

The sand and gravel areas are home to a number of species that are adept at camouflage, and may not be immediately apparent. One approach is just to settle on the sand and concentrate on the area a metre or so in front of you. Often species like dragonets, gobies and dabs will eventually begin to reveal themselves with movement, and will normally become increasingly inquisitive. They tend to move in small jumps and jerks, stopping momentarily to inspect you, which is the moment to take your photograph.

There are larger species more confident of their camouflage, and more likely just to watch you come closer once found. The largest of these in shallow waters is likely to be the monkfish or angler fish, which has amazing camouflage and is content to sit on the bottom gently waving its lure to attract unsuspecting prey. Some particularly large specimens will attract numerous small or juvenile fish, which swim among the lures above the fish's mouth, and are ignored in the sure knowledge that they will attract a much larger meal. Other sand hunters include plaice, turbot and thornback, and blond rays which are often found close to estuaries, digging for crustaceans in the silt.

Closer to the border between reef and sand you may also encounter small schools of red and grey mullet, sand eels (which attract the voracious pollack) and red gurnards, although the latter tend to appear more often at dusk or at night. In the spring and summer months you will begin to spot groups of juvenile cuttlefish no more than 24 mm (1 in) in length. There are many sandy coves where squadrons of juvenile and adult cuttlefish can be found shoaling together, and the seabed will be peppered with them showing off their camouflage skills. So don't ignore the sandy areas – they can prove to be almost as productive as the reef itself.

Offshore reefs

The geology of this area has produced many spectacular offshore reefs, rising steeply from the seabed, and each displaying unique characteristics. At the end of the peninsula, Land's End reaches out into the often wild waters of the Atlantic. Close by is the infamous Runnel Stone, which is reputed to have wrecked more than 27 ships. The Runnel Stone is in fact an extensive area of reefs and pinnacles, which lost its only surface-breaking feature to the last vessel wrecked on the Stone itself, the *City of Westminster*, in 1923. The reef is now marked by a buoy, within sight of Land's End and the Longships reef lighthouse to the south. It is open to Atlantic oceanic conditions, so to explore the reef here means waiting for the best tides and weather conditions, as even in good weather there is normally a swell to contend with. Local knowledge is essential as the tides are vicious and sometimes unpredictable, and the weather can change very quickly. But under the right conditions the 'Stone' and surrounding reefs are simply stunning.

The topography of these offshore reefs is immensely rugged, the geology granite and serpentine, which produces a bright yellow, heavy sand that settles quickly after storms. As there are no river outfalls to upset the water clarity, visibility underwater is often excellent. These ingredients are perfect for a dense proliferation of encrusting marine organisms, which in turn attract fish that enjoy the shelter provided by the reef, and perhaps dwell in the sand or prefer the flow of the tide to bring them food. Each reef complex offers a rich microcosm of marine life in temperate waters. Due to the strong currents at many locations, only the hardiest of seaweeds are able to take hold and thrive. The clearer water also enables the kelp canopy to extend down to 15–18 m (50–60 ft) in places, a little less where the reef walls are particularly sheer, and provide shelter and habitat for a wide variety of marine life both sedentary and mobile. Sponges abound, and the first signs of jewel and daisy anemones can be found in water as little as 3 m (10 ft) deep, in almost every colour imaginable, from vivid yellows to deep purples, reds and oranges. Looking up towards the kelp line, graceful plumose anemones can be seen extended, sifting the current for nutrients, and in among them are still more of the smaller daisy and dahlia anemones. These are interspersed with clusters of oaten pipe hydroids reaching out to grasp nourishment from the current. Inspecting these hydroids closely often reveals two or three species of colourful nudibranchs feeding on them, particularly in spring when they are reproducing. Remaining space on the rock surface is mostly occupied by tunicates and masses of feather stars and brittle stars, again seemingly coloured in every hue.

Exploring the walls in the shallows will reveal countless nooks, crannies and ledges, home to familiar inshore species such as crabs, squat lobsters, blennies, shannies and prawns, most of which are both inquisitive and co-operative. Scorpion fish and the nest-building corkwing wrasse are also common here, and in the spring there will be an abundance of spider crabs picking their way among the kelp stypes. Look carefully at the stypes to find cling fish and pipefish taking advantage of their camouflage. As you go deeper, the reef system offers walls, gullies and plateaus which support an astounding wealth of marine life, even playing host to the occasional sub-tropical visitor such as trigger fish and sun fish. It is common to encounter large shoals of mackerel, bass and pollack, which show little fear of visitors to their world. On many offshore reefs among the rocks are the remains of the numerous wrecks, some so close or overlapping that it is difficult to tell when you swim from one to another.

Open waters

You might want to leave the bustling activity of the reefs, and move offshore to explore life in the open waters of our coastline, which still harbour schools of fish despite heavy commercial fishing. However, in my experience, encountering a shoal of mackerel or herring in the water, or capturing their image, is probably more a matter of luck than of planning. I have often leapt from the deck of a boat with enthusiasm to chase a shoal of mackerel with my camera, which can not only be seen clearly on an echo sounder, but are also coming up to the deck on hooks as I submerge, yet when I reach my target depth I am on my own again.

The frantic reproduction and burst of life propagated by the arrival of spring also produces the first plankton blooms as the top few metres of water begin to rise in temperature. Plankton consists of microscopic and just visible collections of juvenile species (zooplankton), which begin their life in the water column, and algae blooms (phytoplankton), all of which are hoping to settle on the reefs and seabed to develop into fish, crustaceans or seaweeds. These plankton blooms are often very obvious when viewed from the shore, for they may be very dense, and can turn the water green or grey, leaving scum lines on the beach as the tide recedes.

There are plankton-feeders out in the open waters, in particular the second largest fish in the ocean. This is the mighty basking shark, which can reach a staggering 10 m (33 ft) in length, and is commonly seen off our shore in May and June. These fearsome-looking fish are in fact totally harmless, and are now a protected species in British waters, having been targeted for generations for their liver oil. It is an awesome experience to swim with these gentle giants, and you should grab the opportunity if it arises. They have been known to come close inshore to feed in less than 2 m (6 ft) of water, when plankton is trapped in a bay like Kennack Sands on the Lizard, or Porthcurno Cove near Land's End.

Jellyfish are another summer visitor. Not all of them will sting the unwary swimmer, although some can be quite painful. They are slower moving than a basking shark, and can look spectacular when viewed against the sun, close to the surface. Other occasional guests include leatherback turtles, which sadly are often found drowned in fishermen's nets, and the sun fish. Sun fish are found in the South Western Approaches and the Bristol Channel, and occasionally turn up in the North Sea during particularly warm summers. Although they laze happily on the surface alongside a boat, they will quickly sound once they become aware of your presence in the water, so you have to be prepared for a fleeting glance unless you are lucky to find a co-operative subject.

Practicalities

Rock-pooling, snorkelling and diving are possible all year round, but the winter months are something of a lottery due to the potentially stormy conditions. Summer is the best time to plan a dive, when the weather is more predictable, but winter can produce amazing water clarity during calm conditions between the storms. Season also affects water temperature, with the coldest months being February and March, after the sea has cooled during the autumn and winter. Sea temperatures can range from 14° to 20°C during the summer, to a chillier 8 to10°C during the winter, so for snorkelling it is wise to wear a light wetsuit to keep warm. If you are diving, a thicker, warmer wetsuit or a drysuit will be required.

Exploring the inshore reefs with basic snorkelling gear is truly worth the effort, but always be cautious of local weather and tidal conditions. Many of the larger beaches in Cornwall have a life guard during the summer months, so be sure to consult them if you are unsure of conditions. If you are exploring more remote coves, then contacting the Coastguard is a wise first step to gain local knowledge and ensure that your explorations are safe. Move slowly, watch carefully, and you will be rewarded with some memorable encounters with Cornwall's rich marine life.

Equipment and image details

The first rule of underwater photography is to keep the water out of your camera! All the pictures in this book were taken with standard land single lens reflex cameras (SLRs), both digital and film, inside bespoke waterproof housings. Most of the images were shot with either a macro/close-up lens or an extreme wide-angle lens behind dedicated ports. The majority were lit with flash to restore the colours that are absorbed by water as the depth increases.

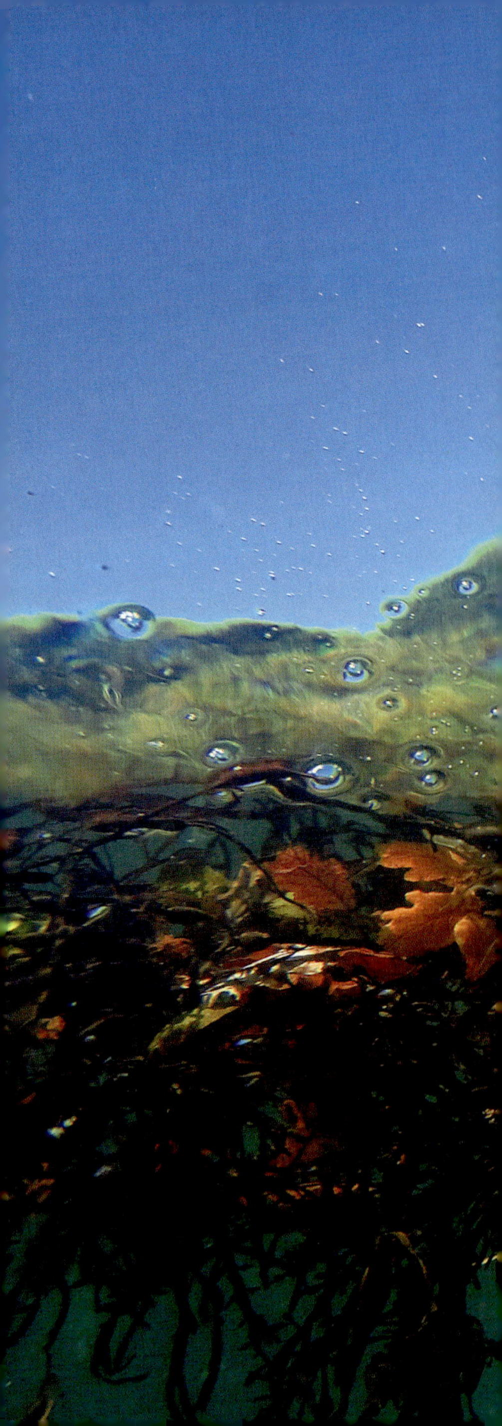

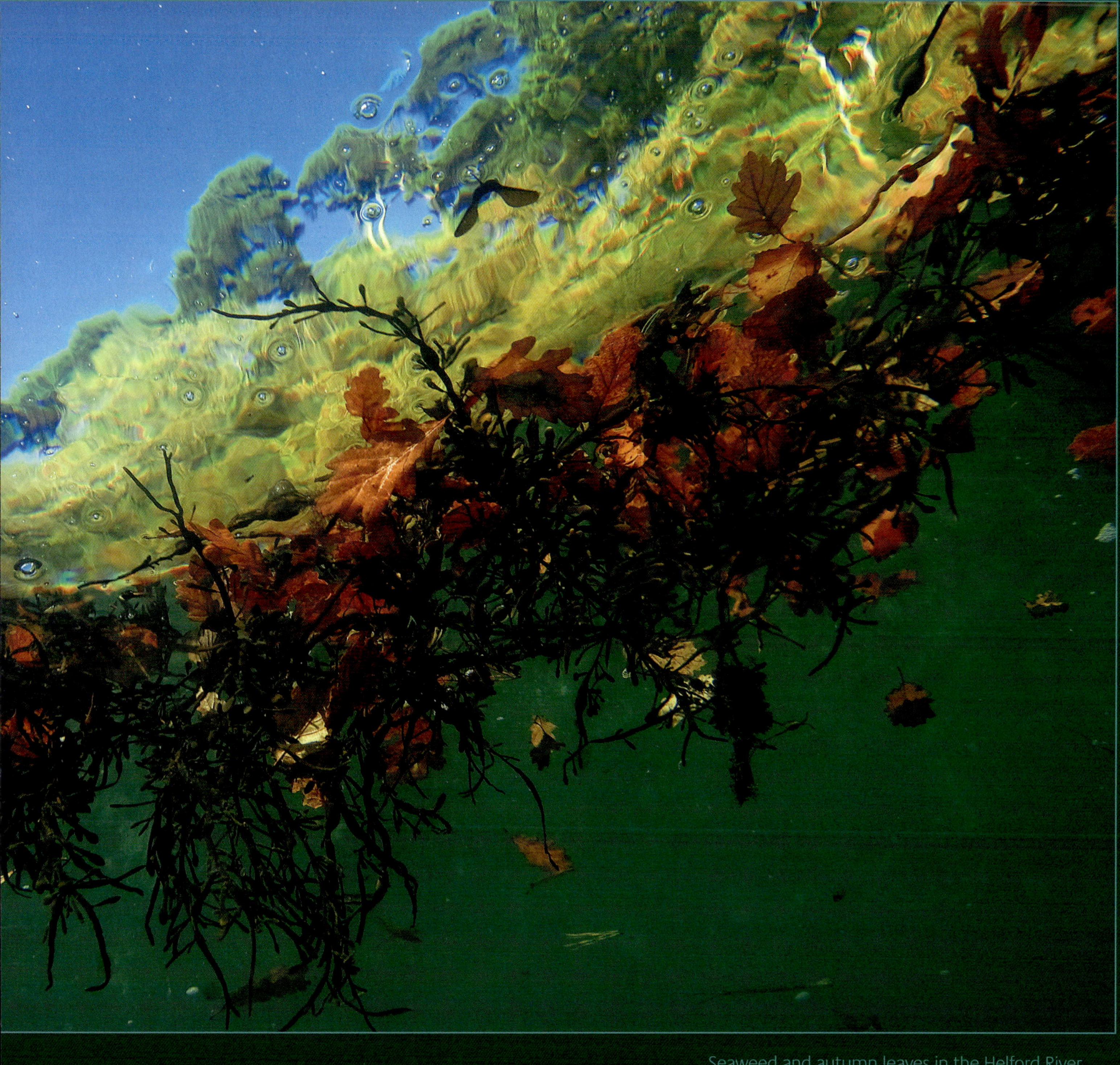

Seaweed and autumn leaves in the Helford River

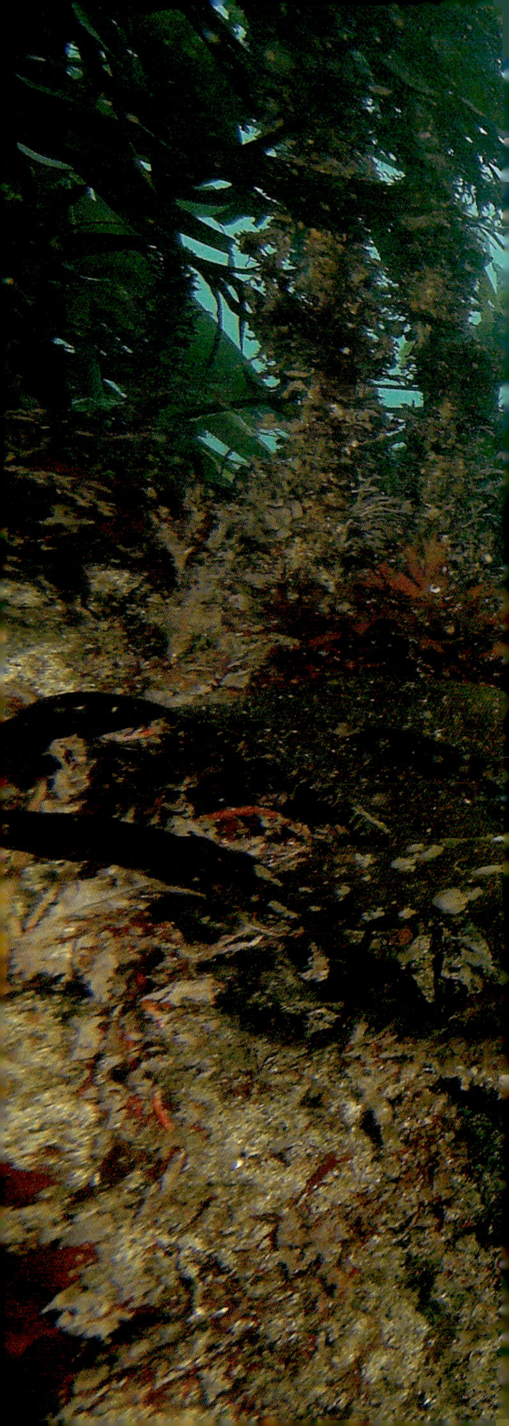

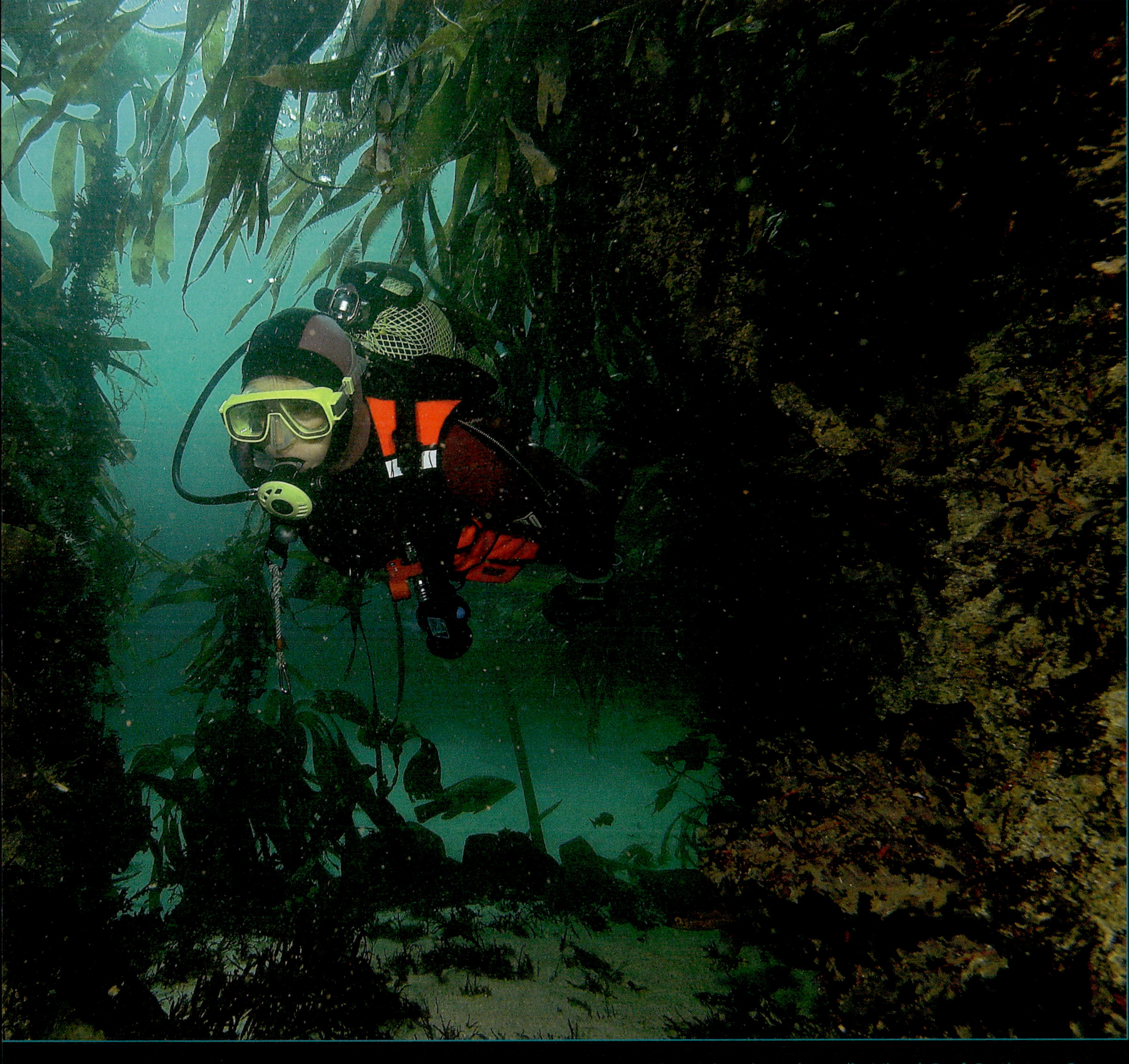

Diver swims through a gully, Minack Reef, Porthcurno Bay

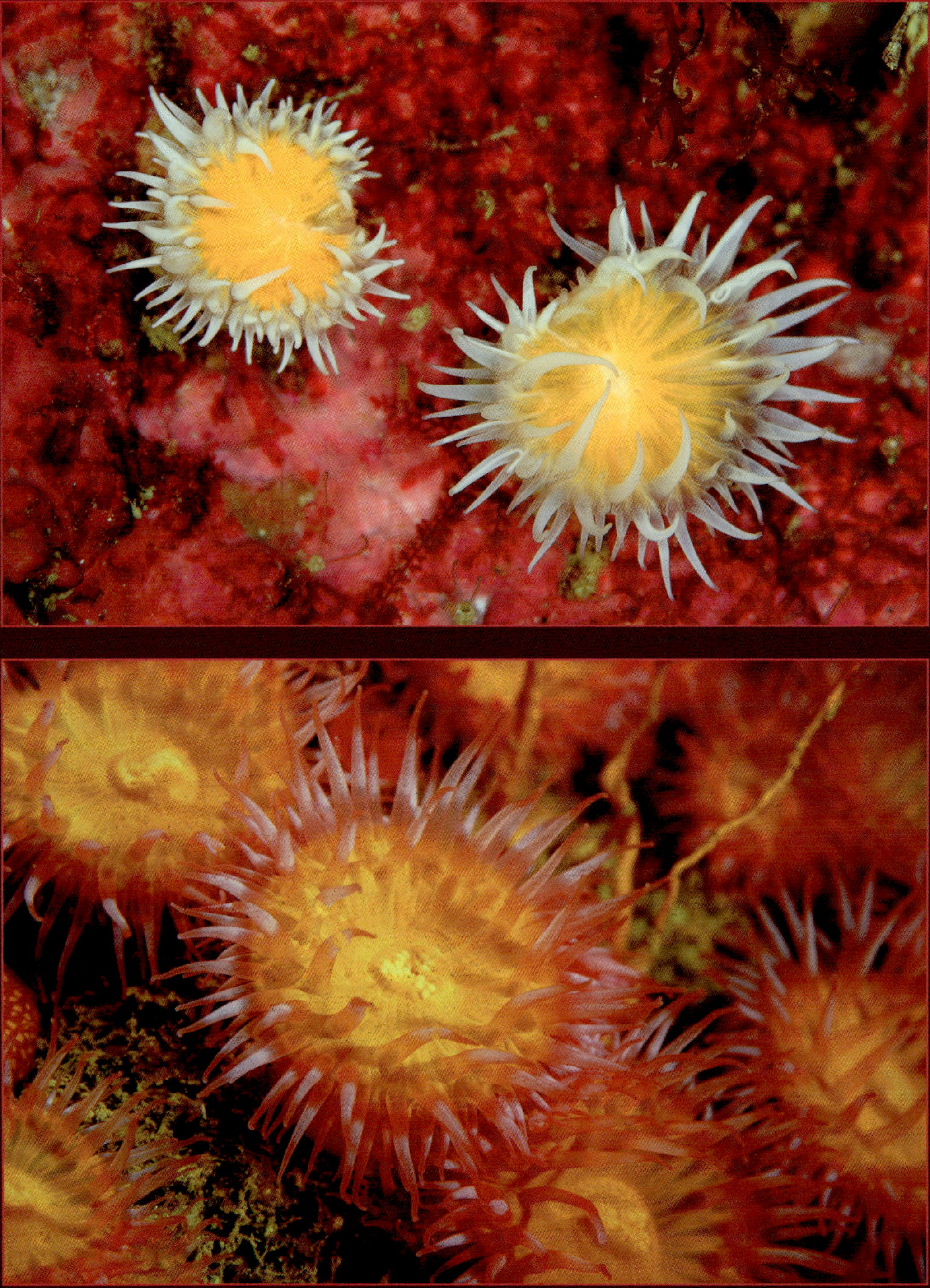

Daisy anemones on red algae (top), and dahlia anemones among hydroids

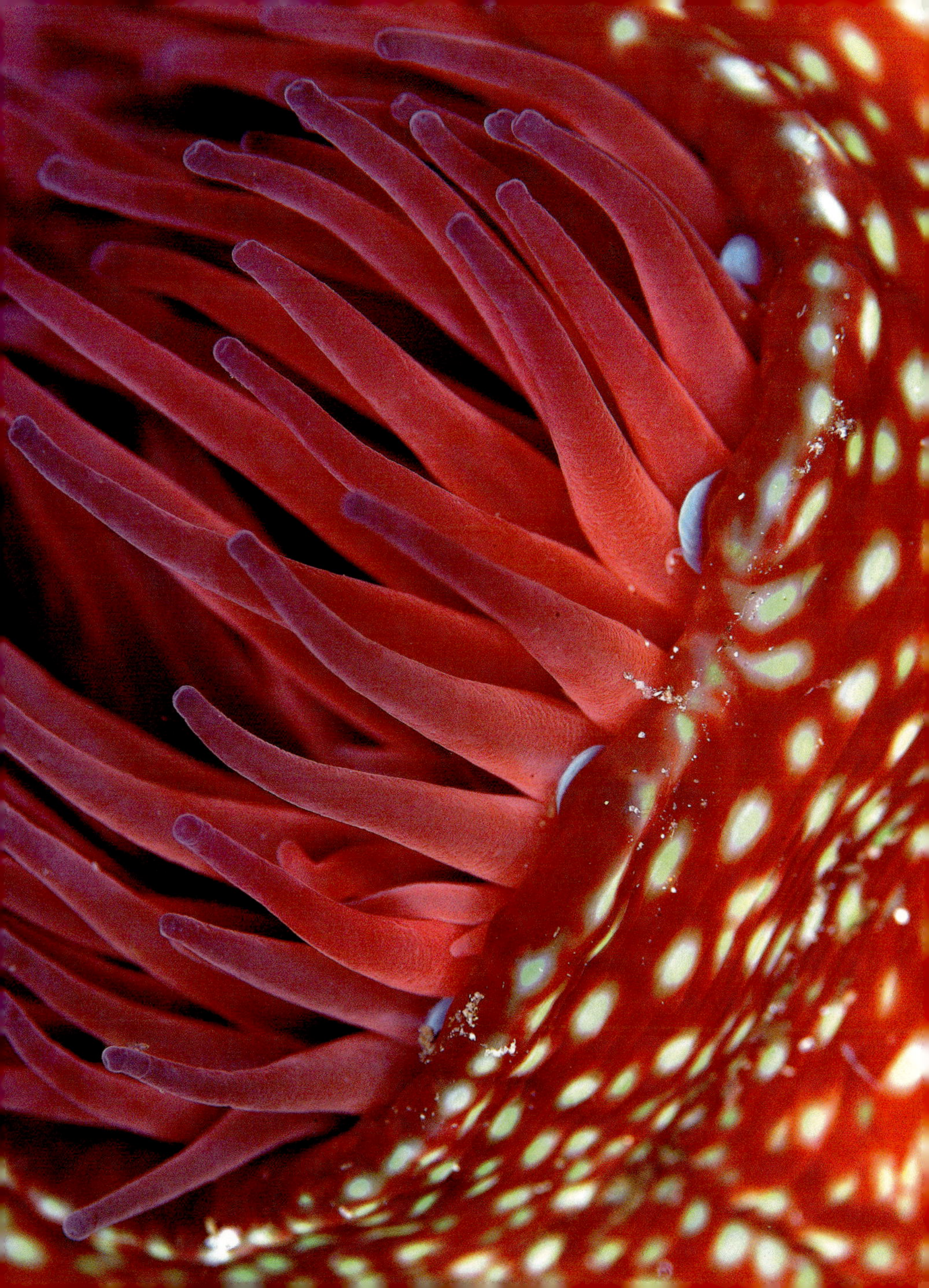

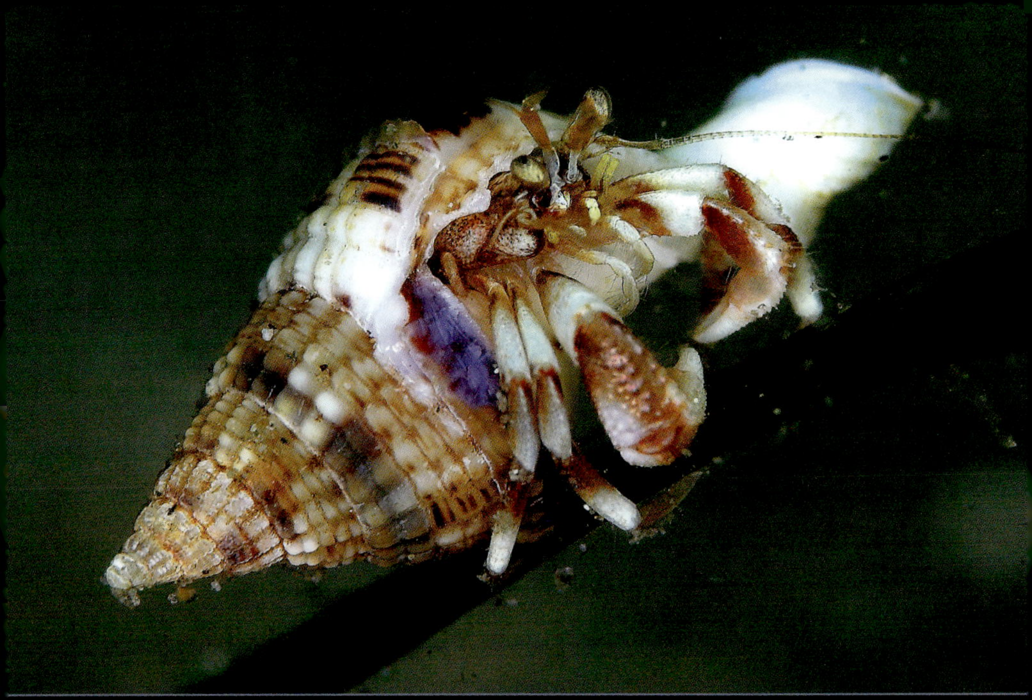

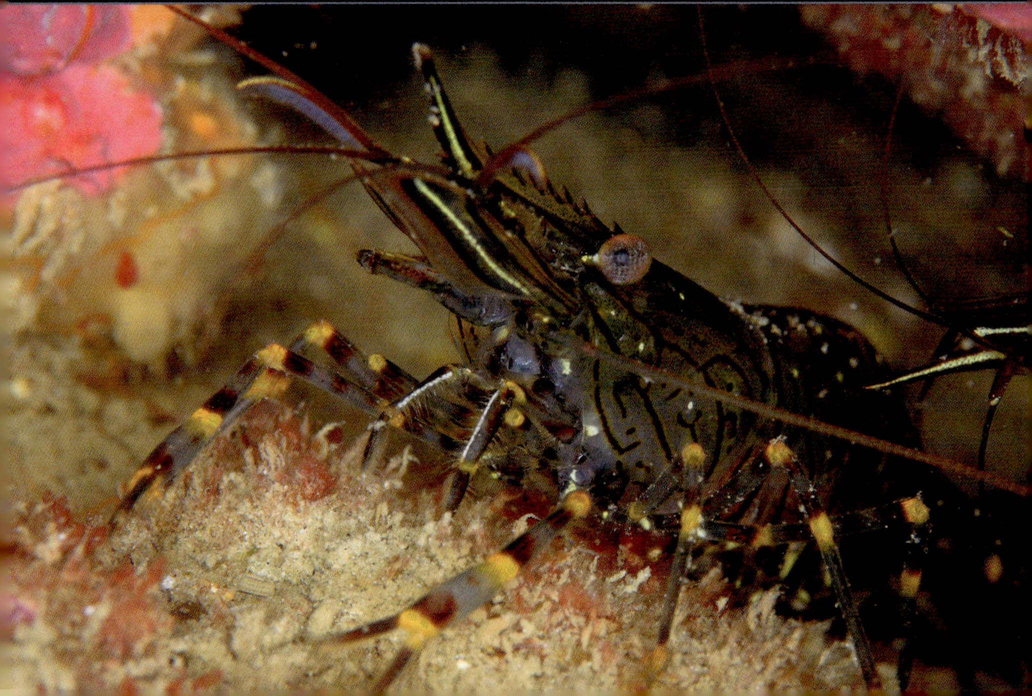

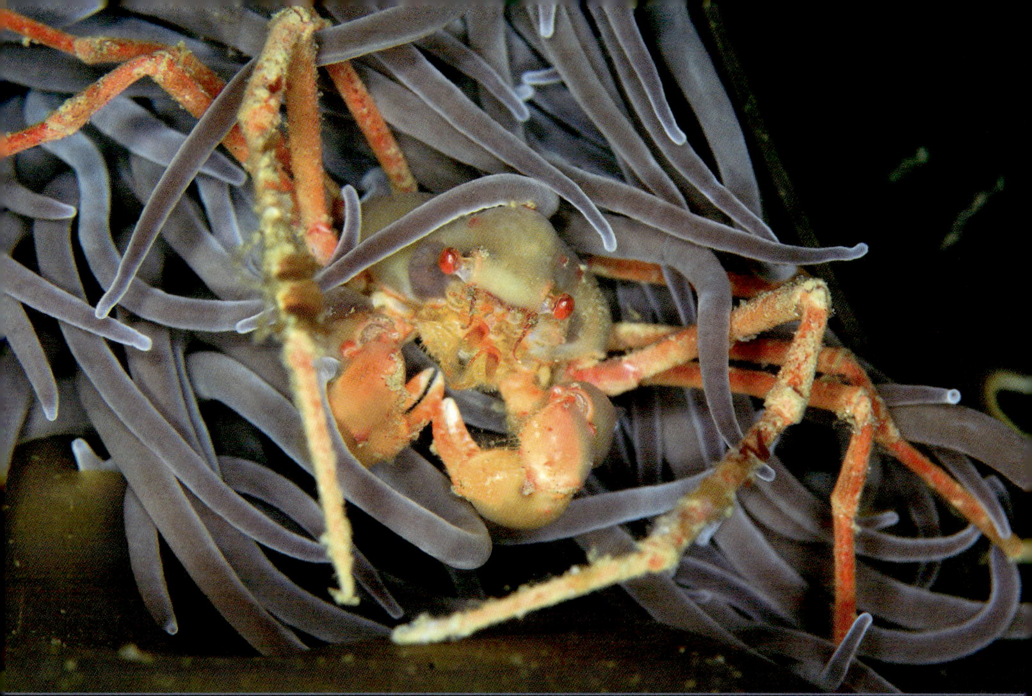

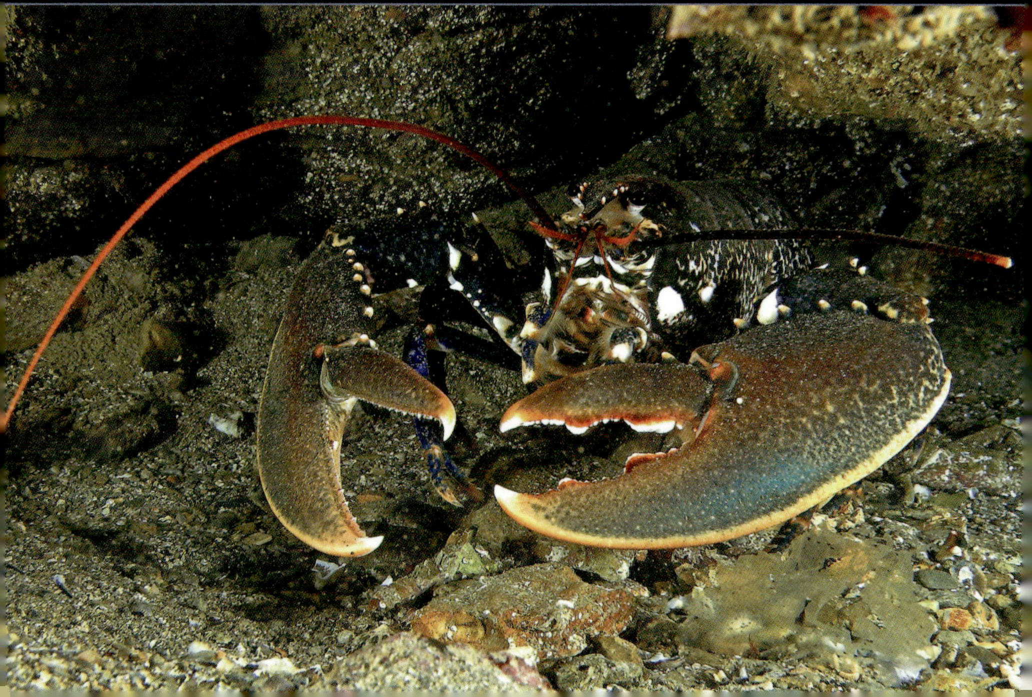

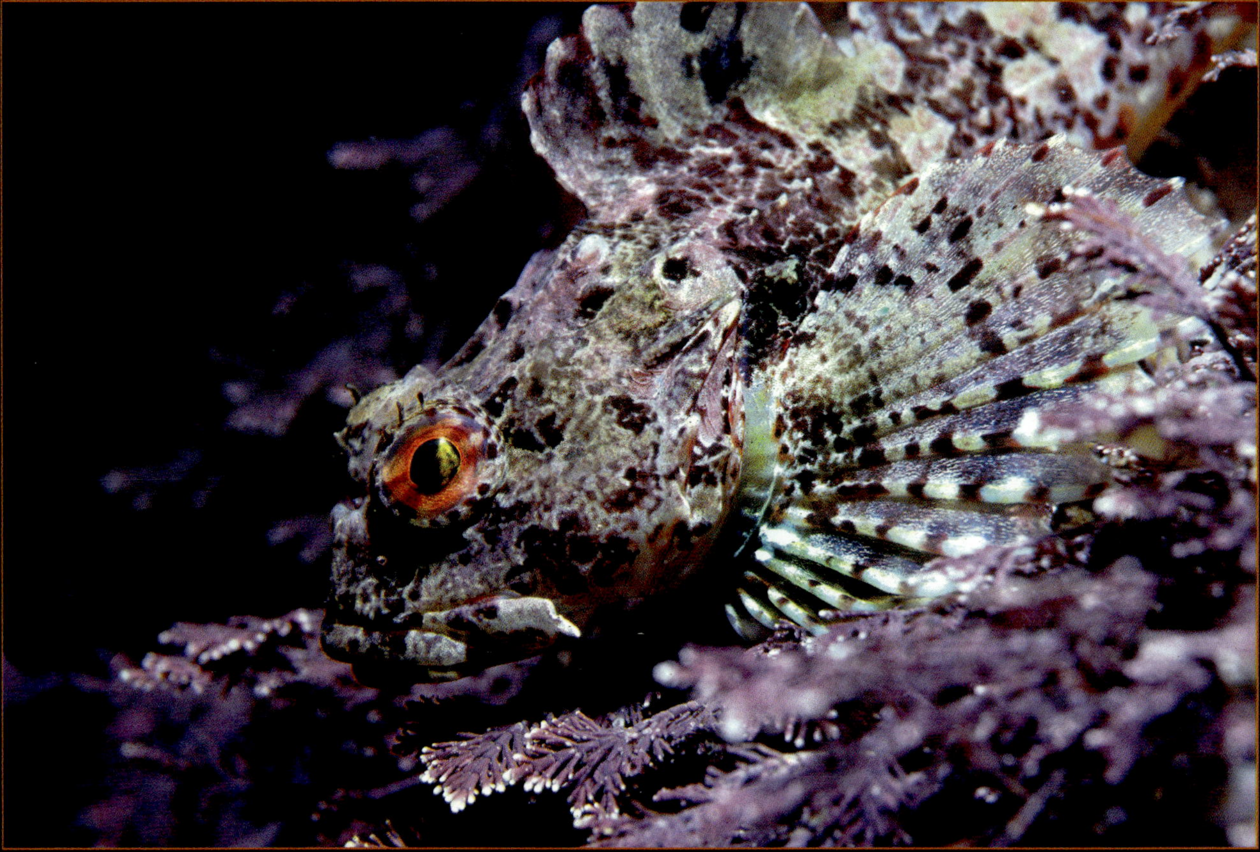

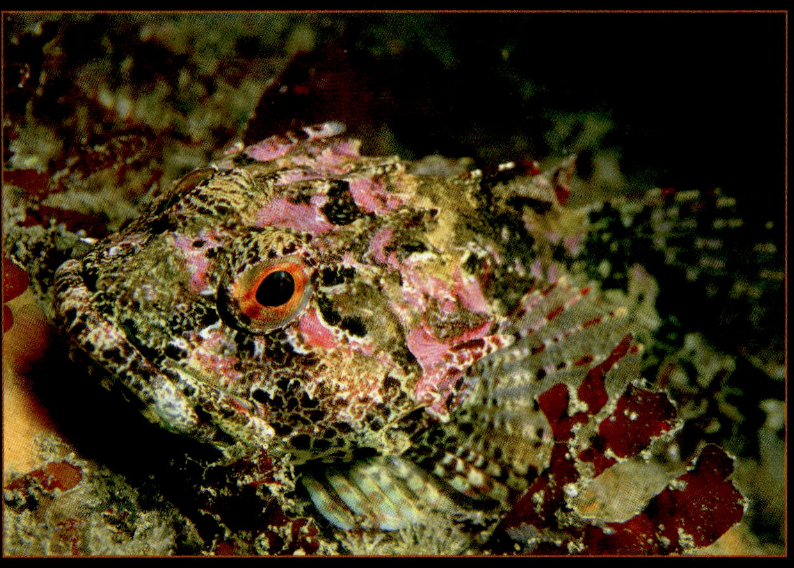

Long-spined scorpion fish (top), and short-spined scorpion fish

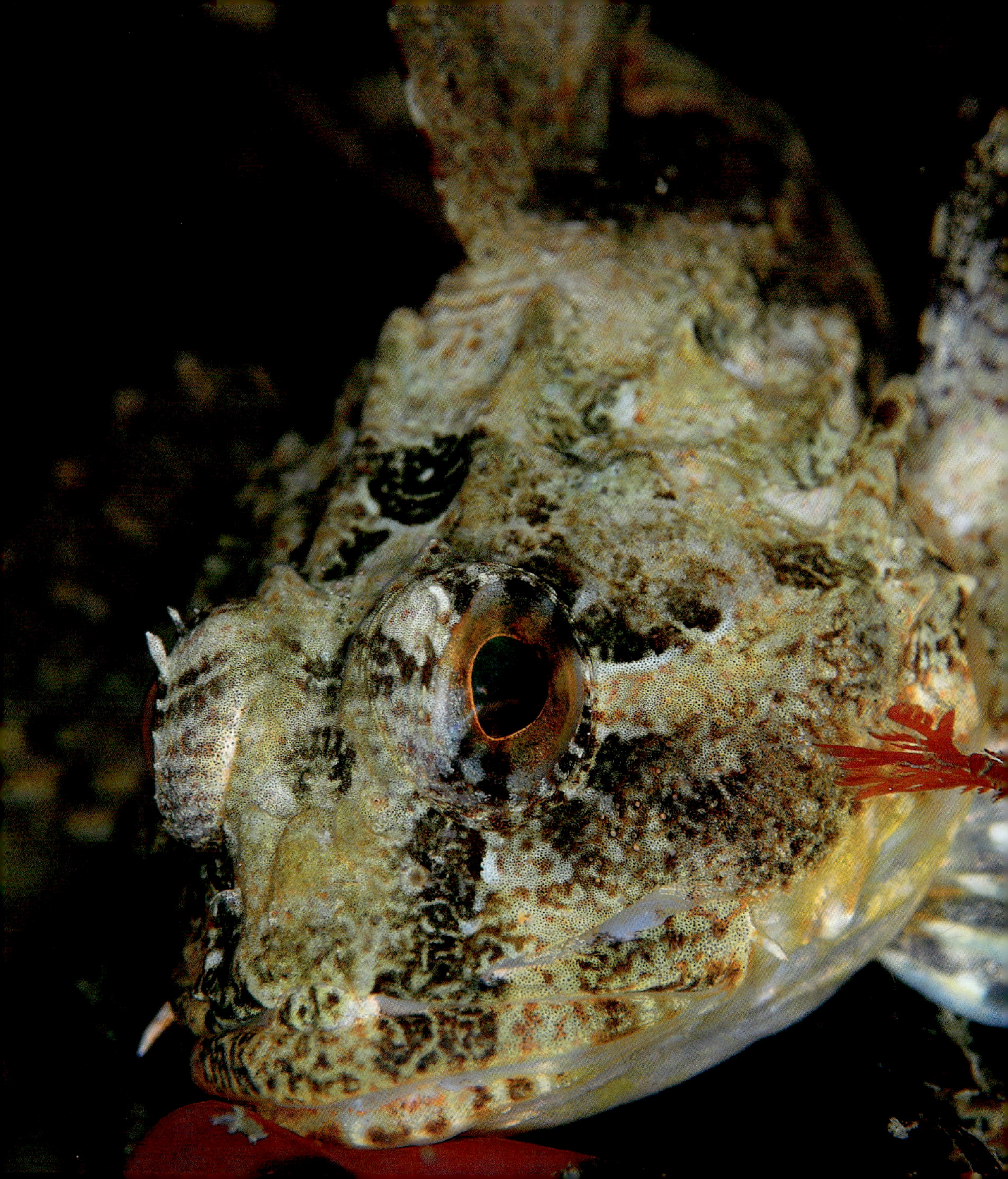

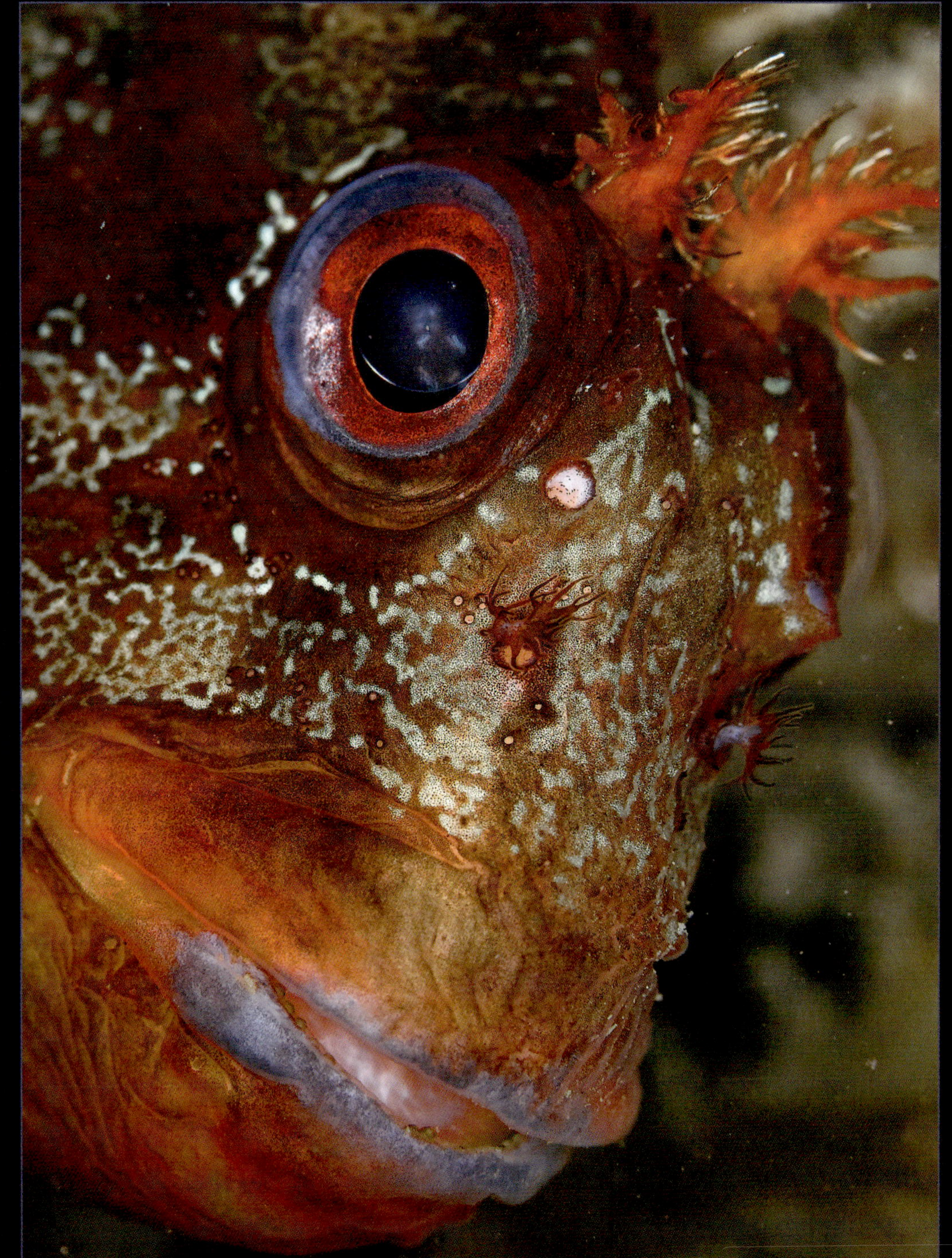

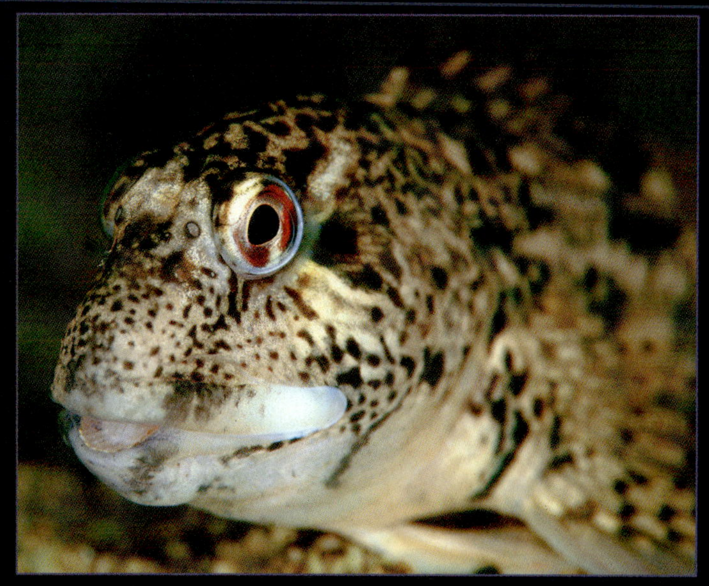

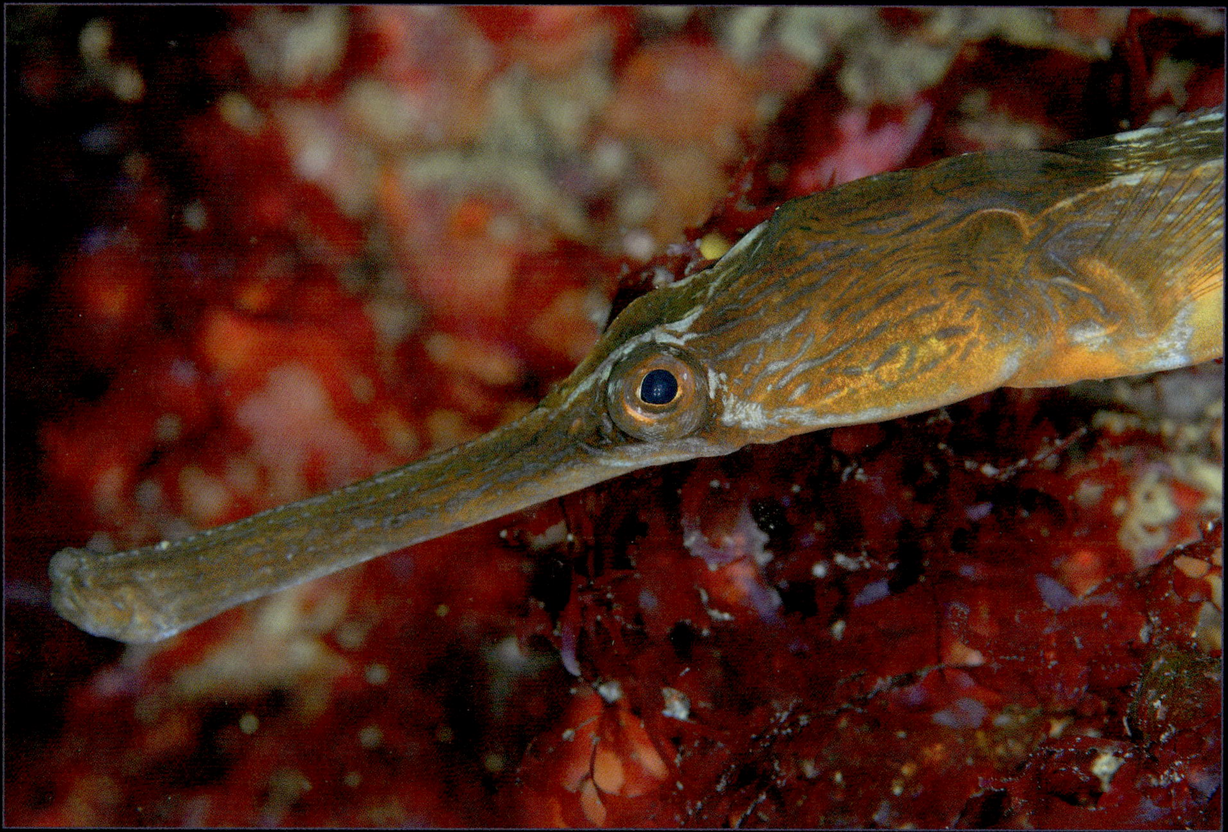

Shanny (top), and greater pipefish

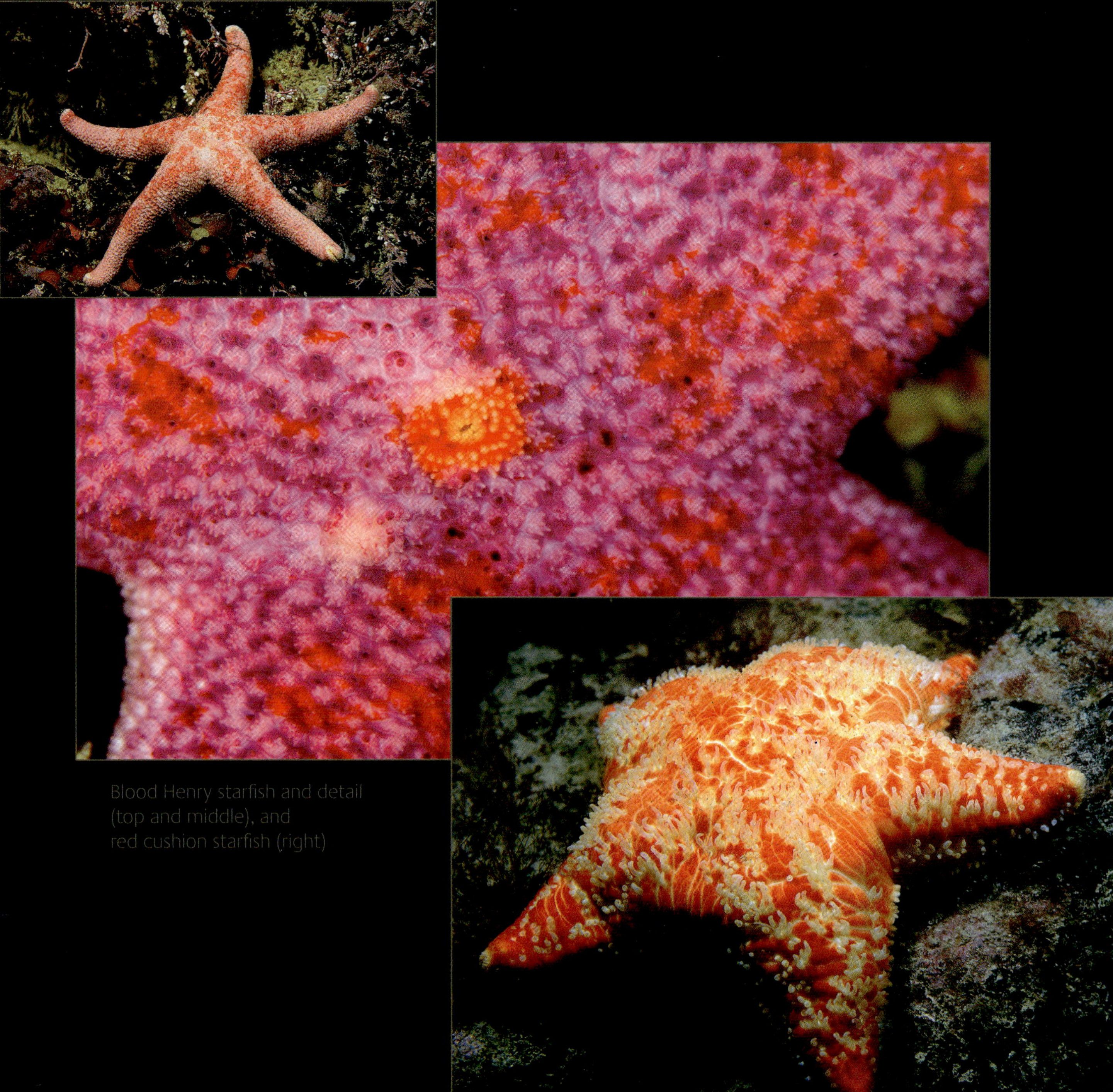

Blood Henry starfish and detail (top and middle), and red cushion starfish (right)

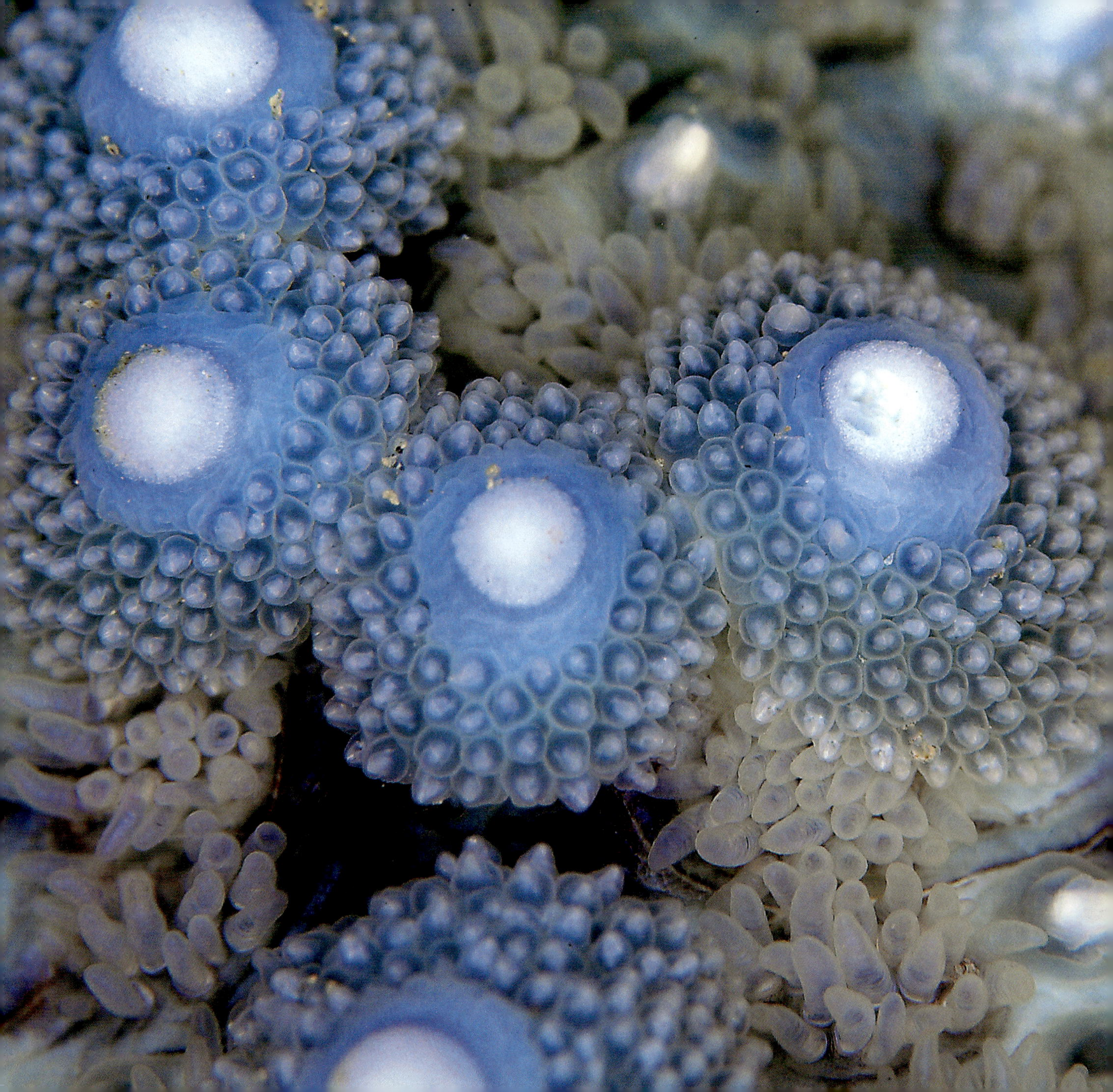

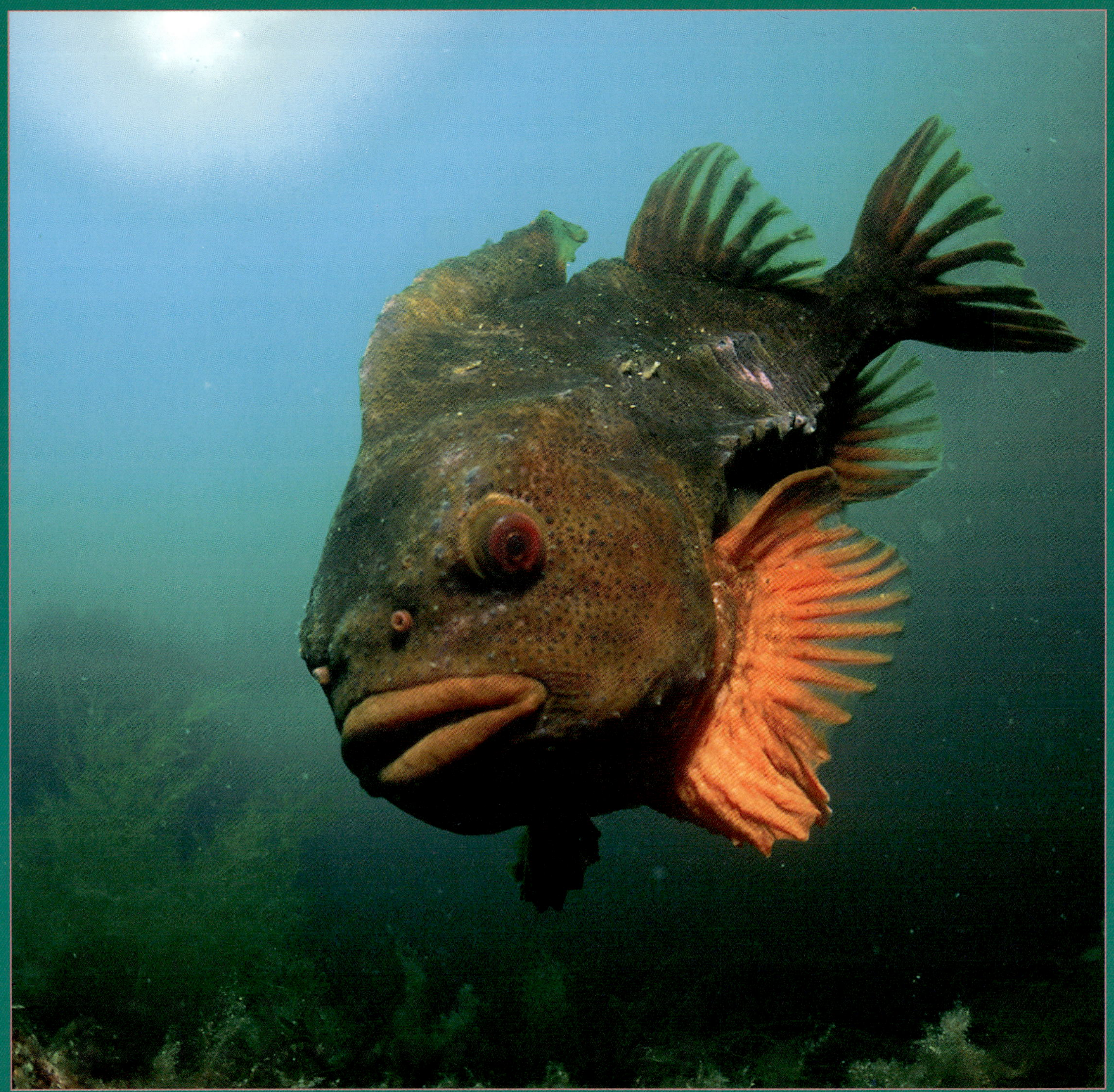

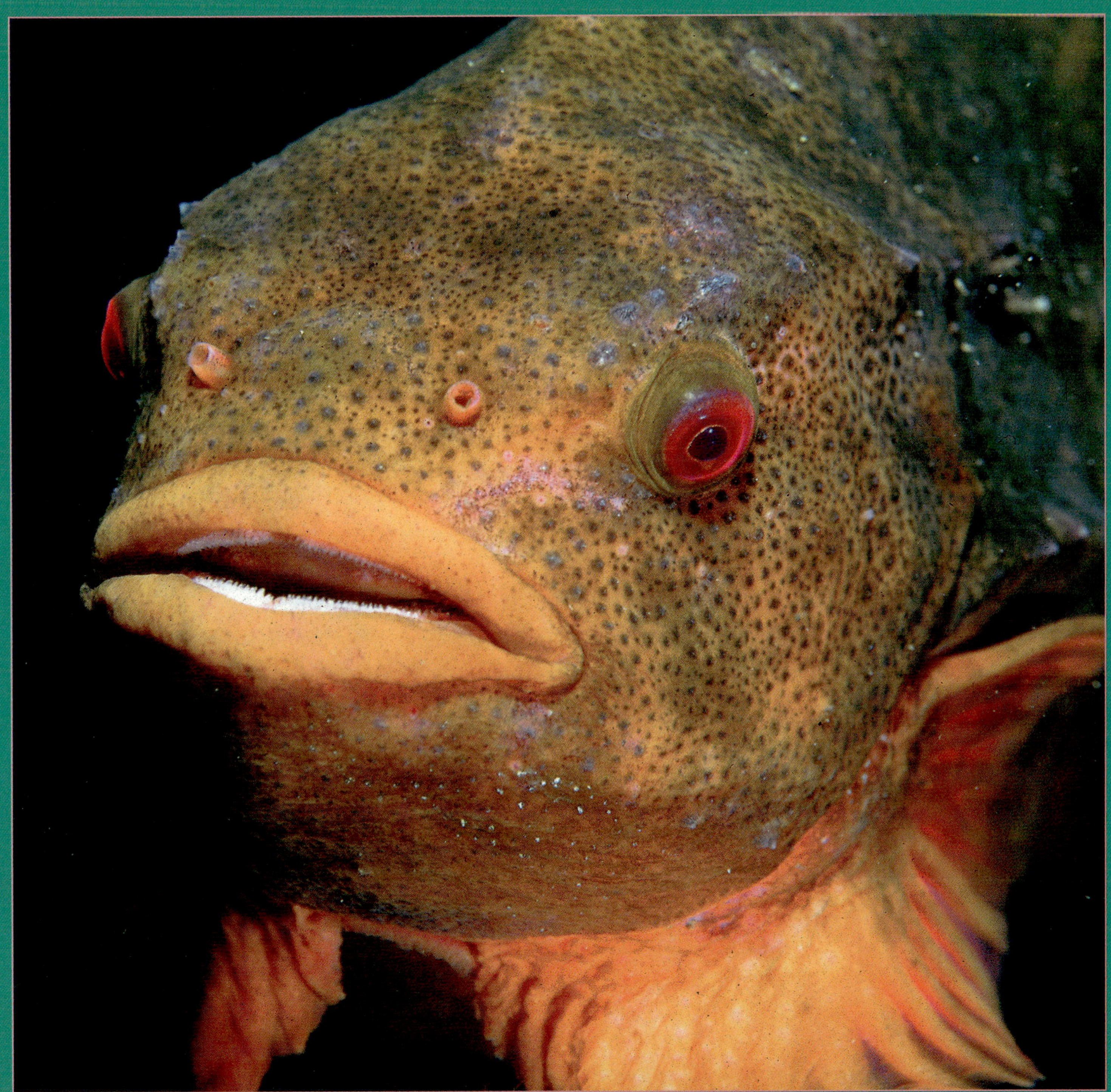

Lumpsucker

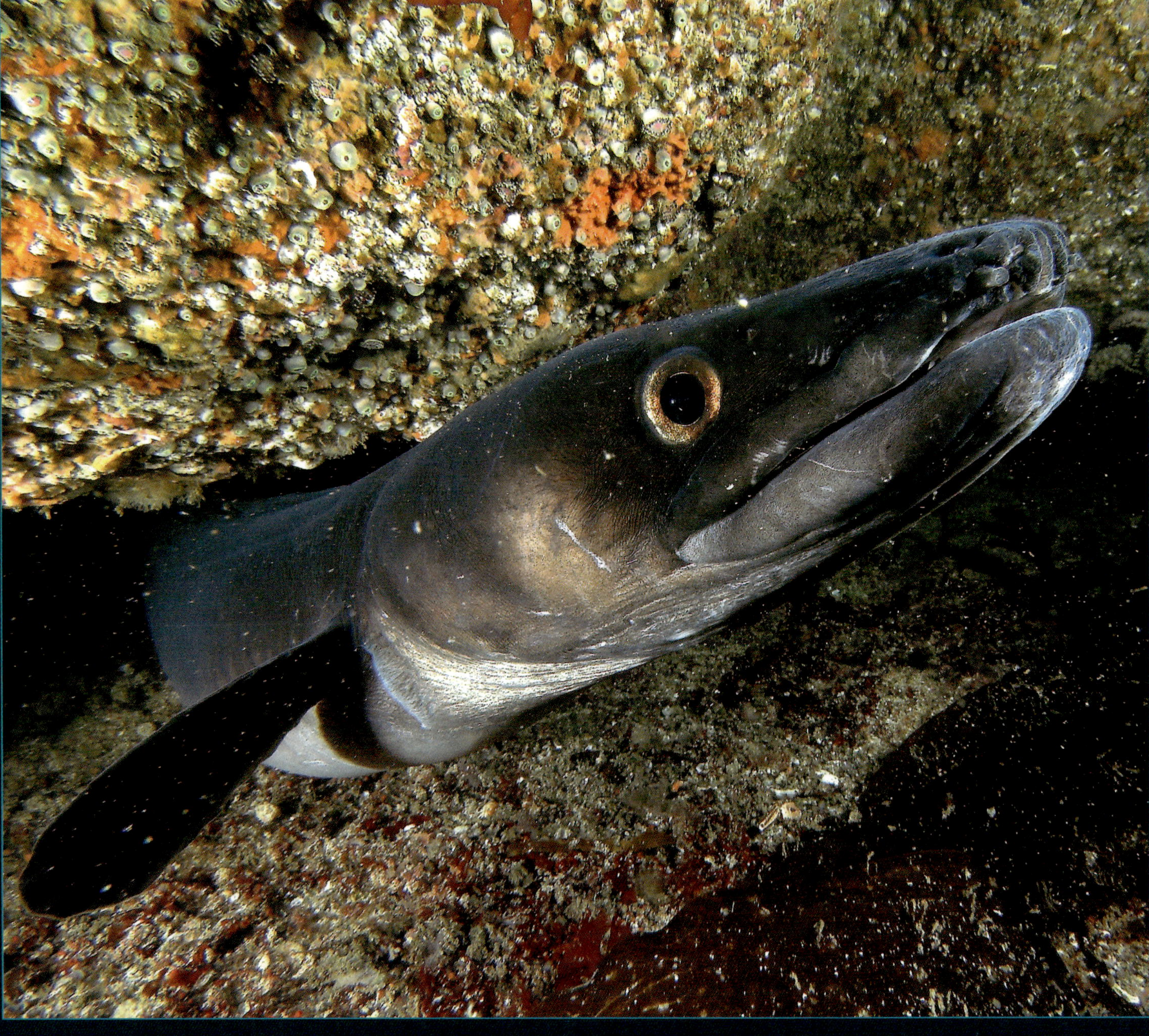
Conger eel

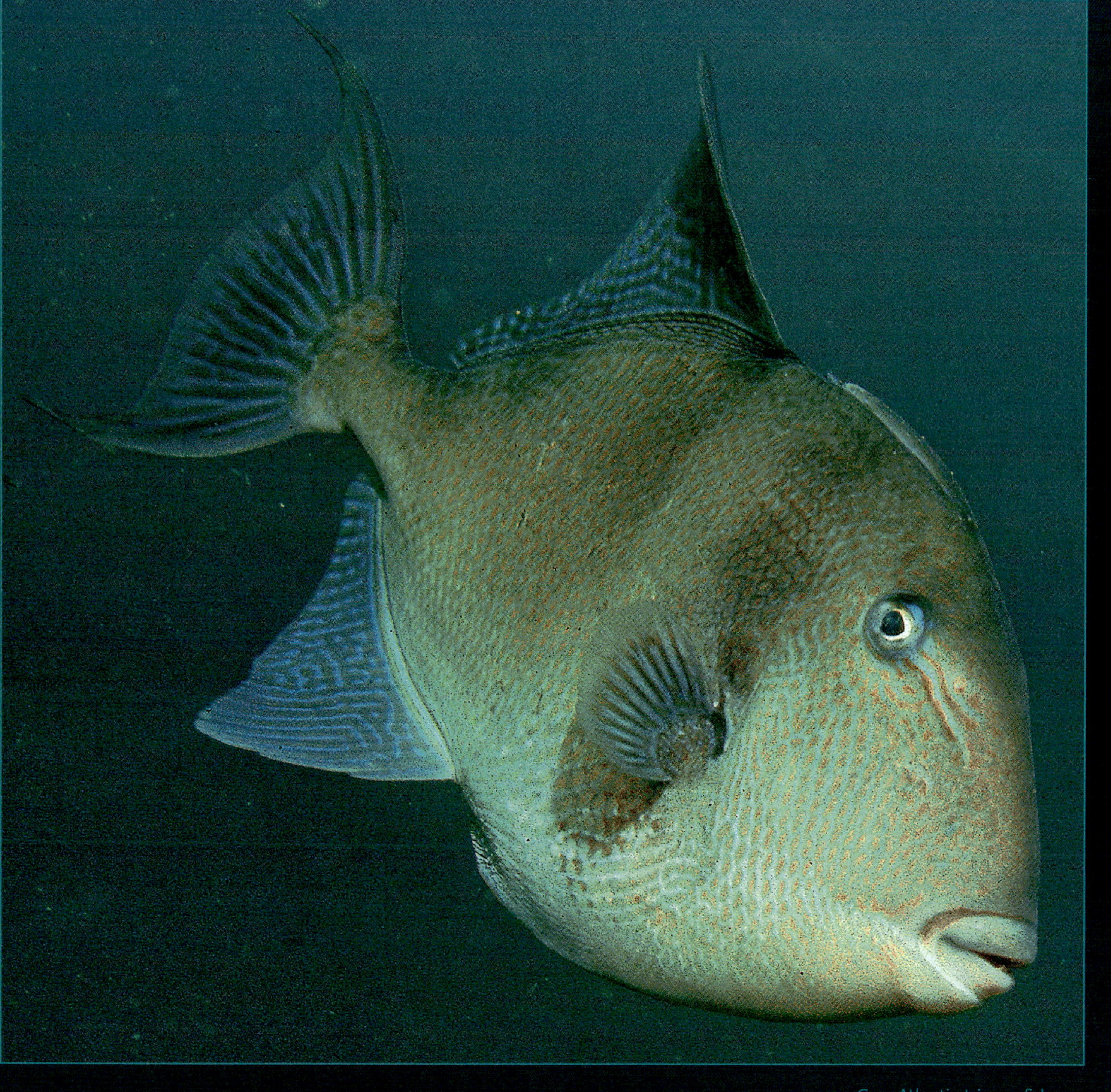

Grey Atlantic trigger fish

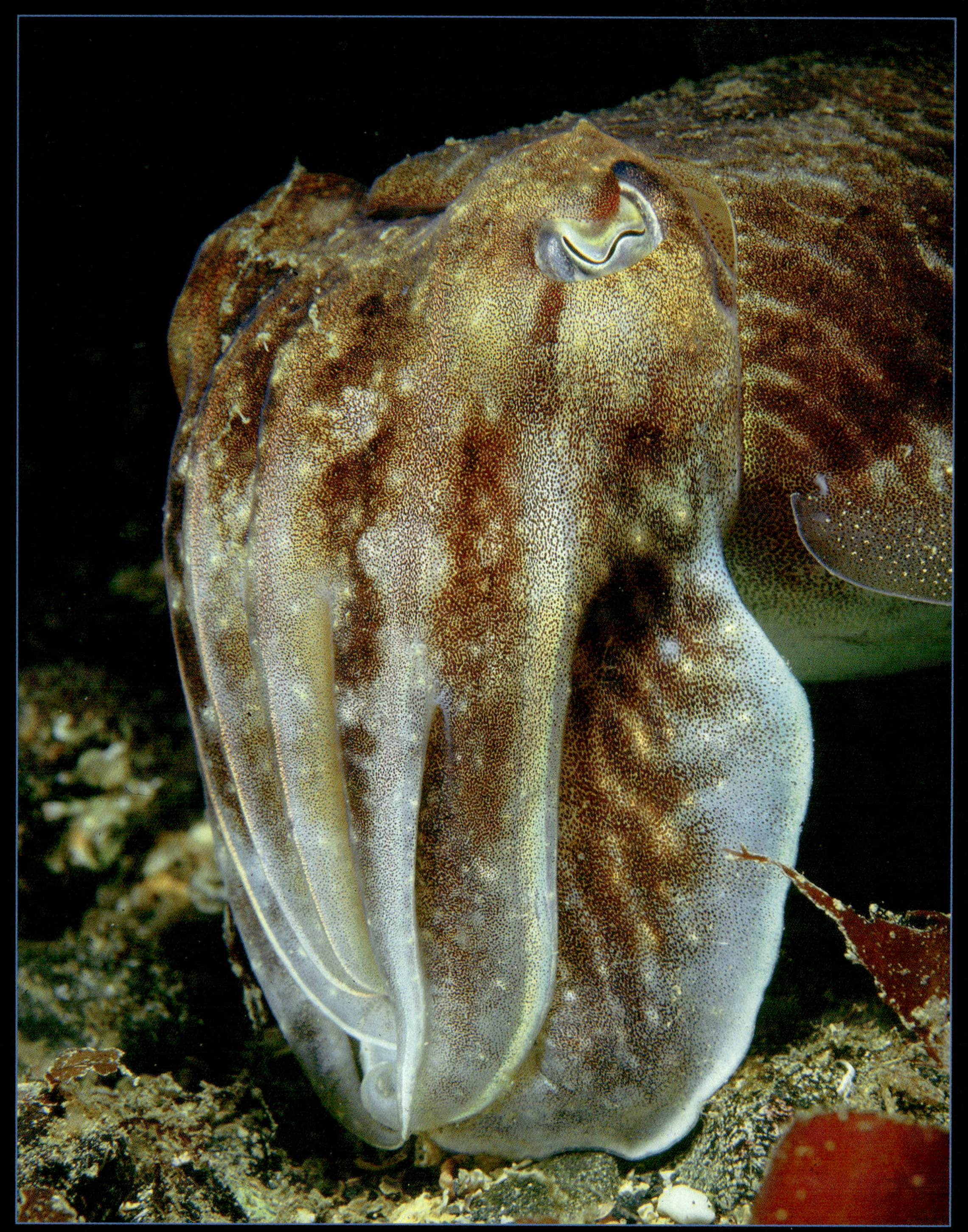

Cuttlefish

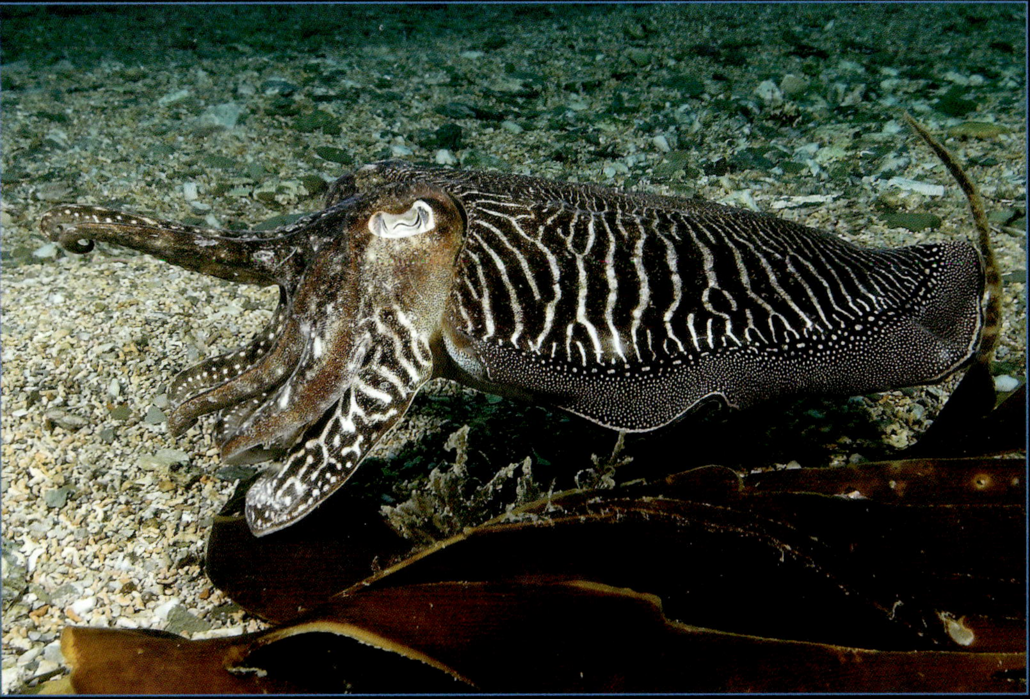

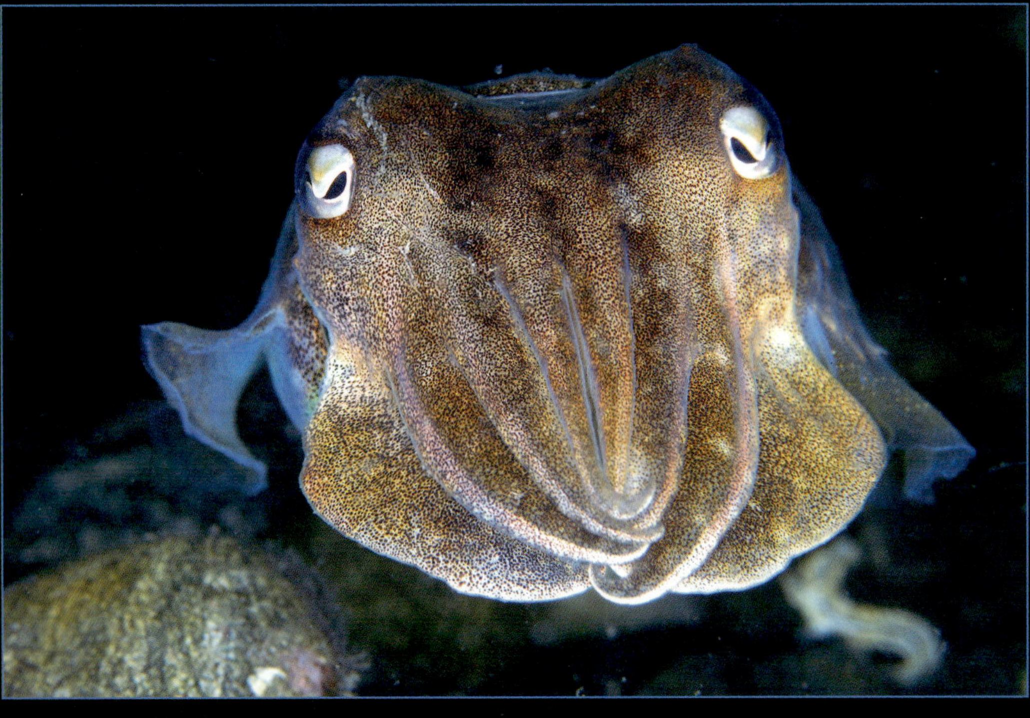

Cuttlefish (top), and juvenile cuttlefish

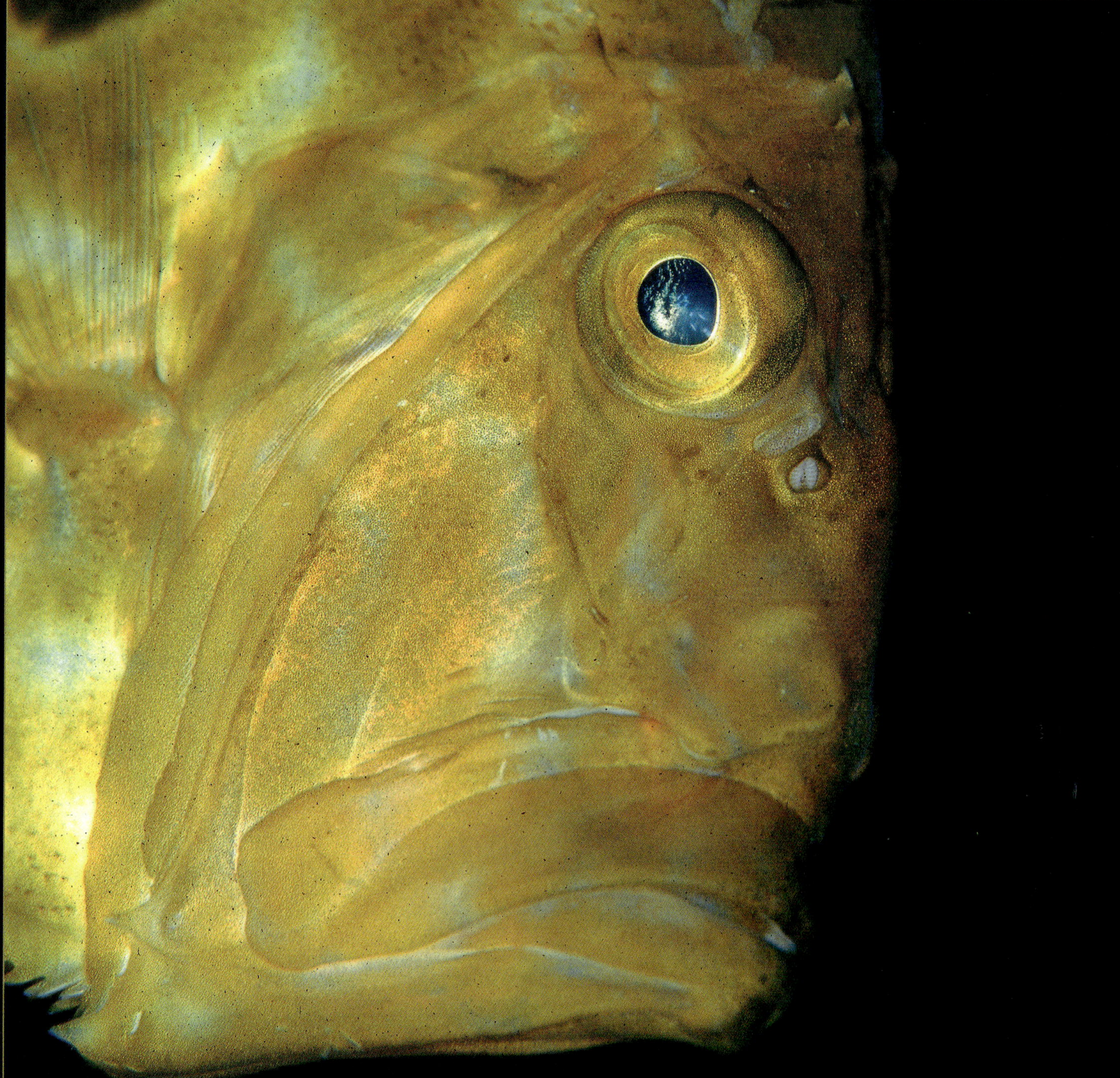

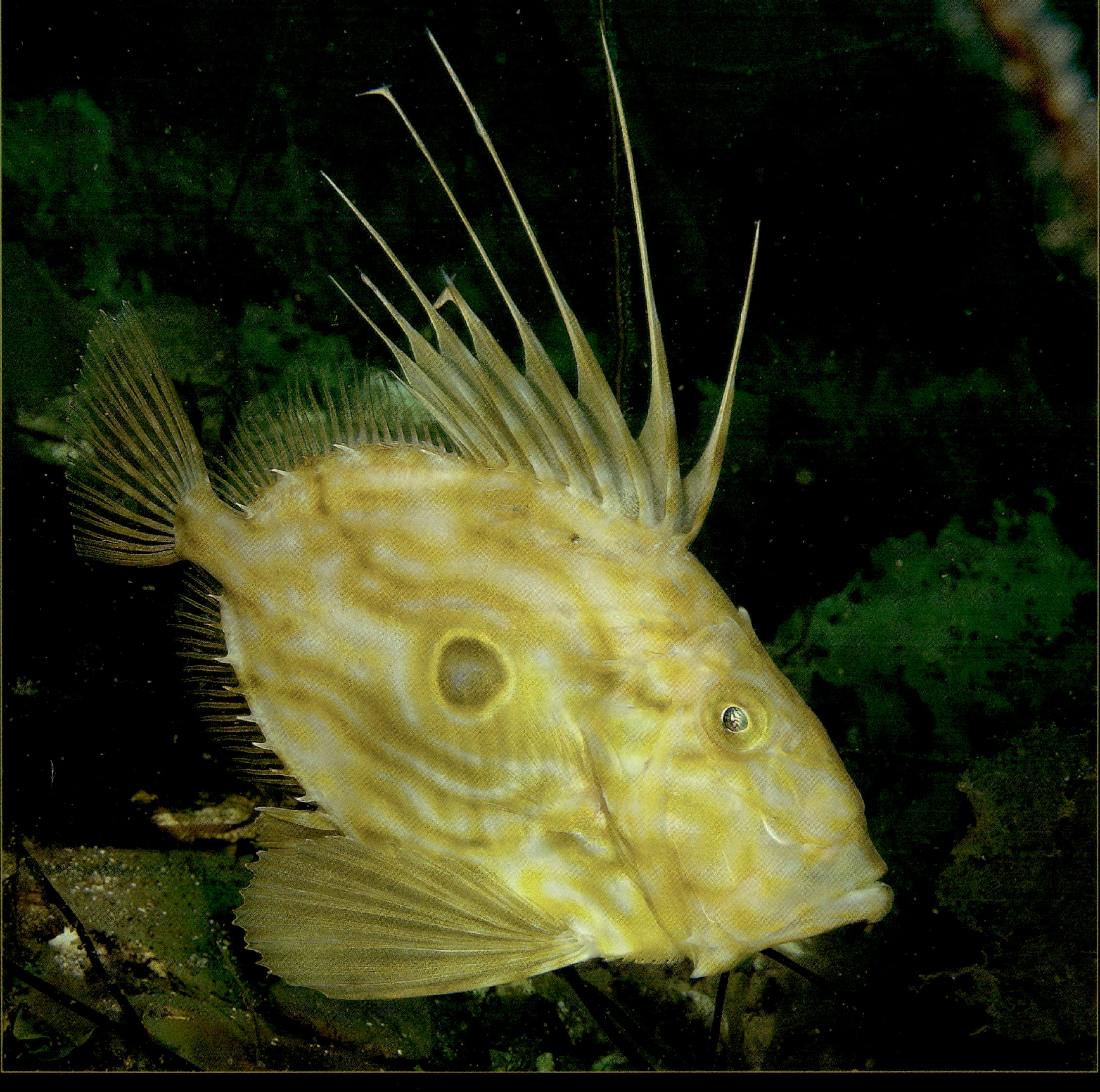

John Dory

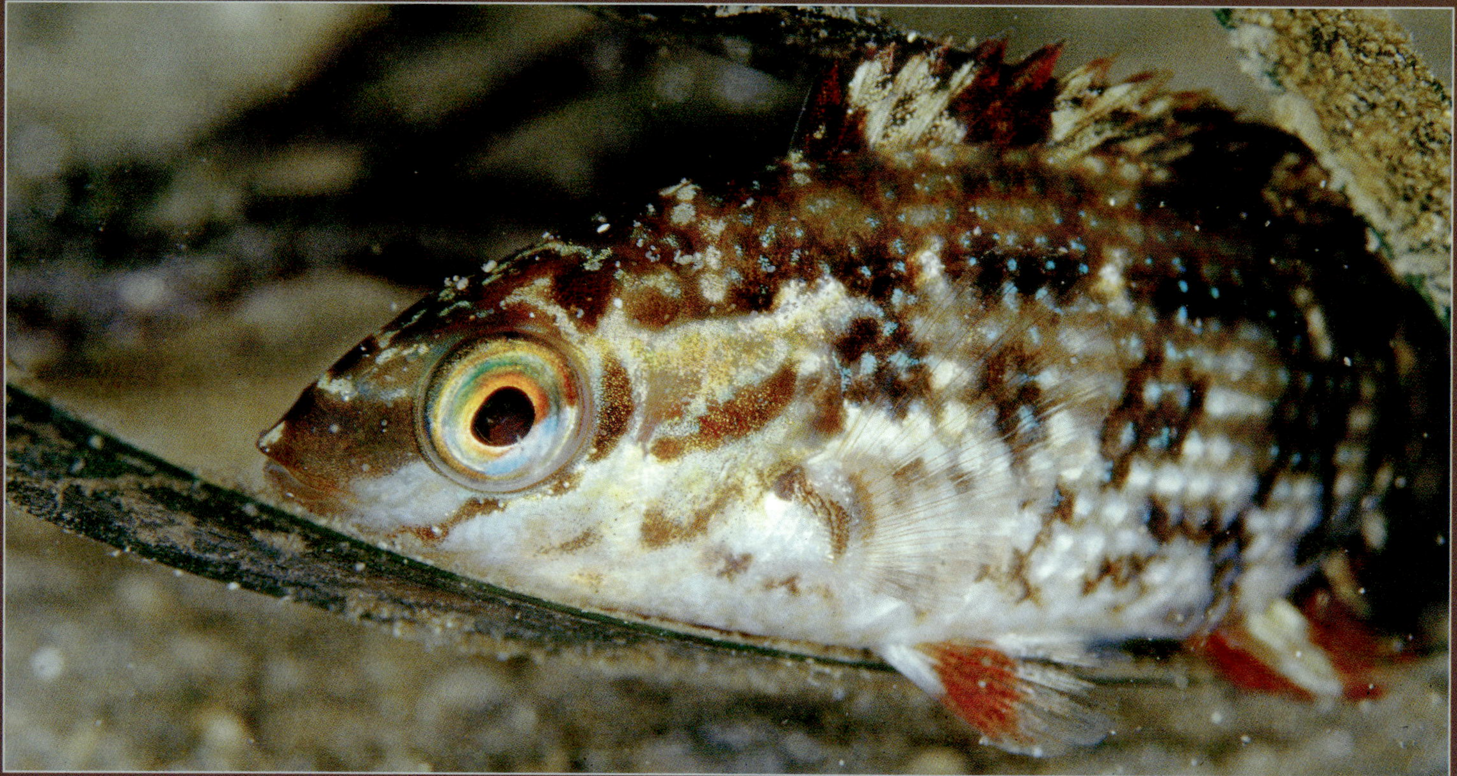

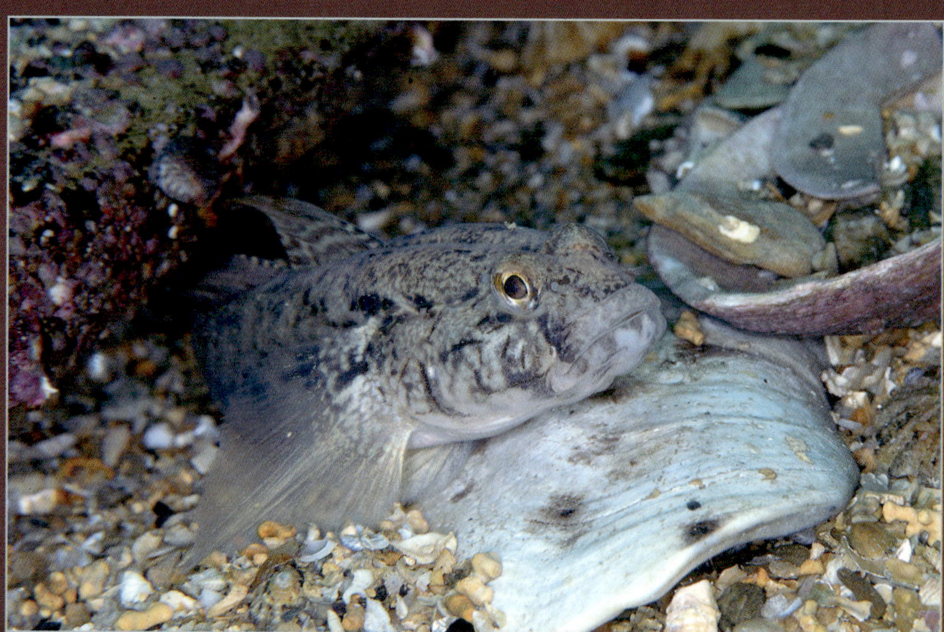

Juvenile corkwing wrasse (top), and black goby

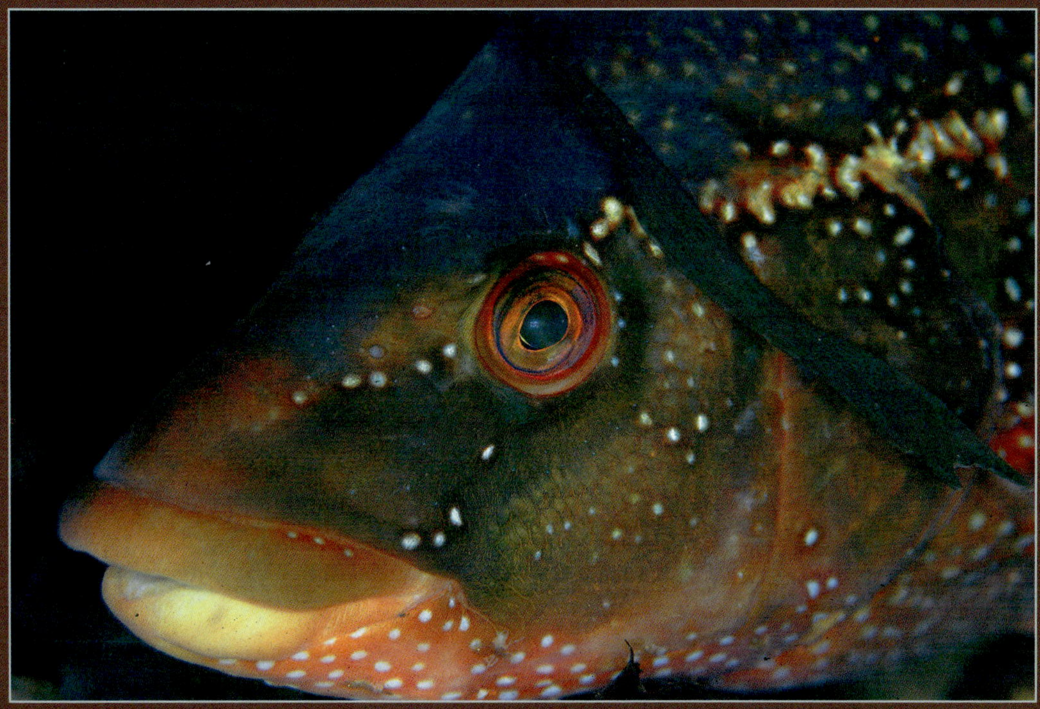

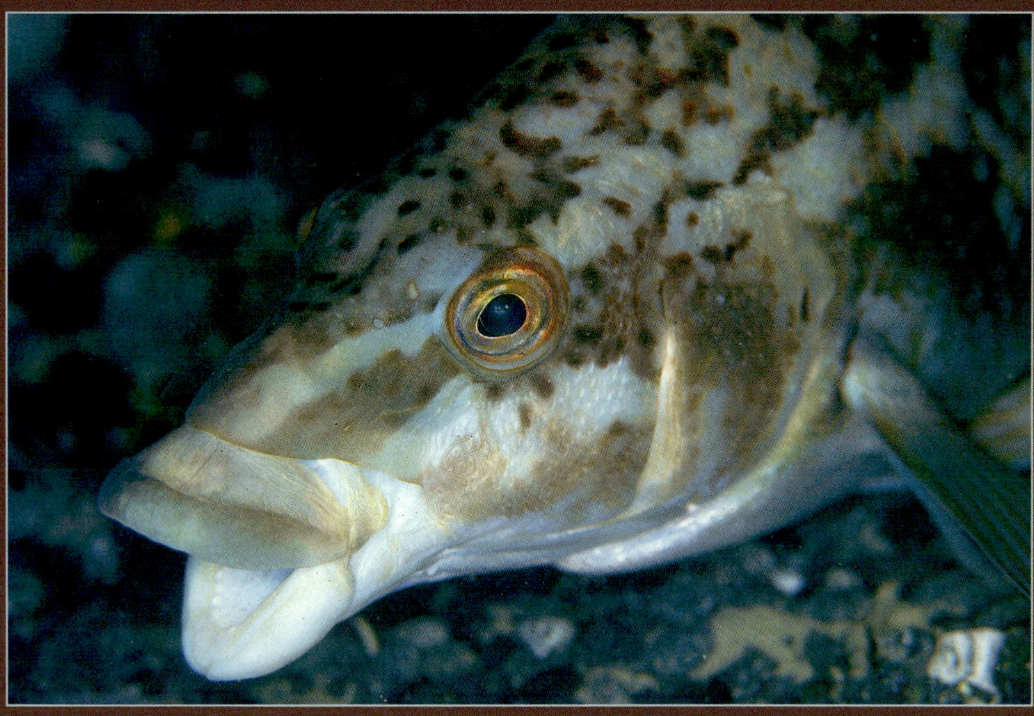

Ballan wrasse (top), and ballan wrasse yawning

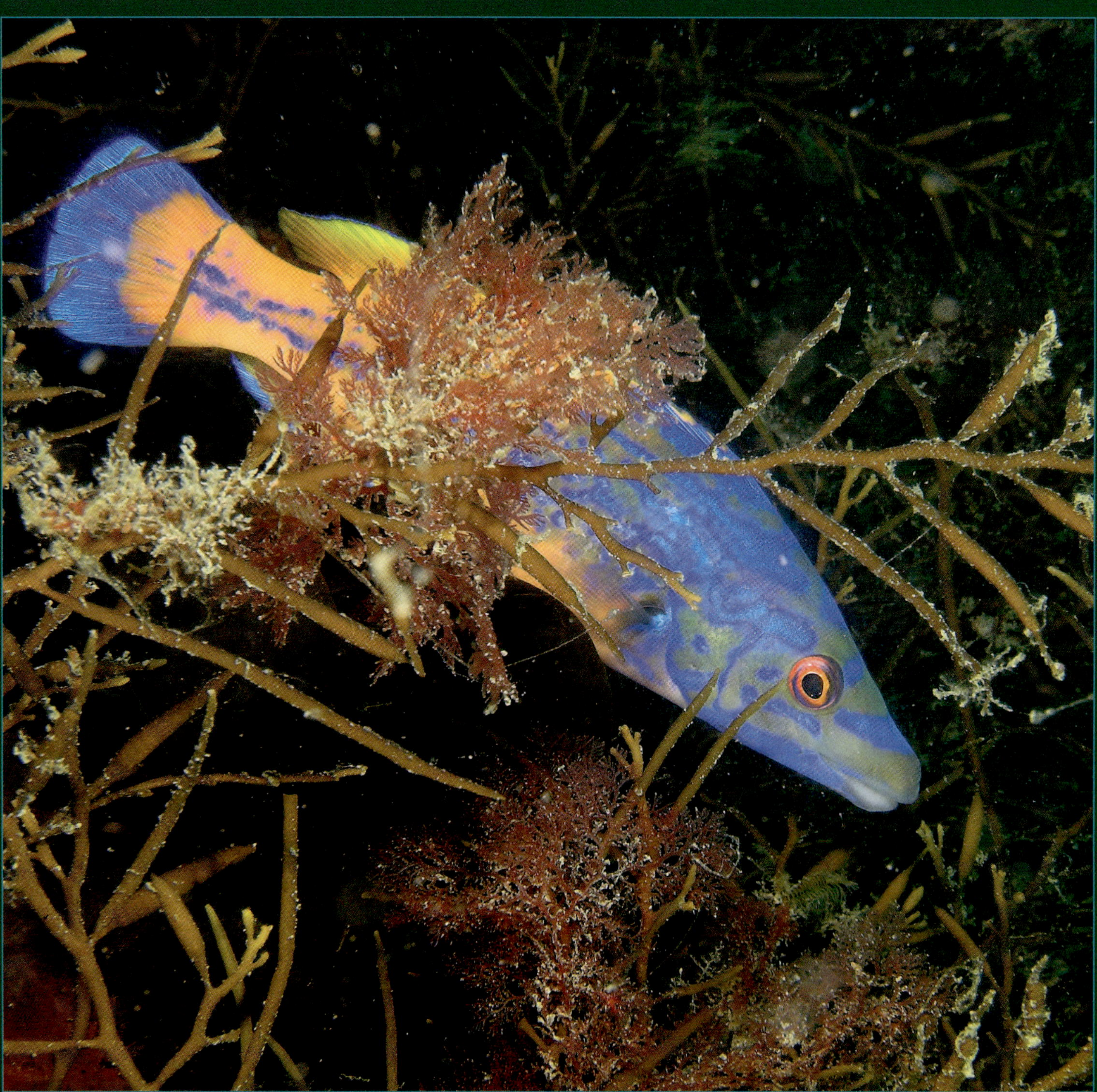

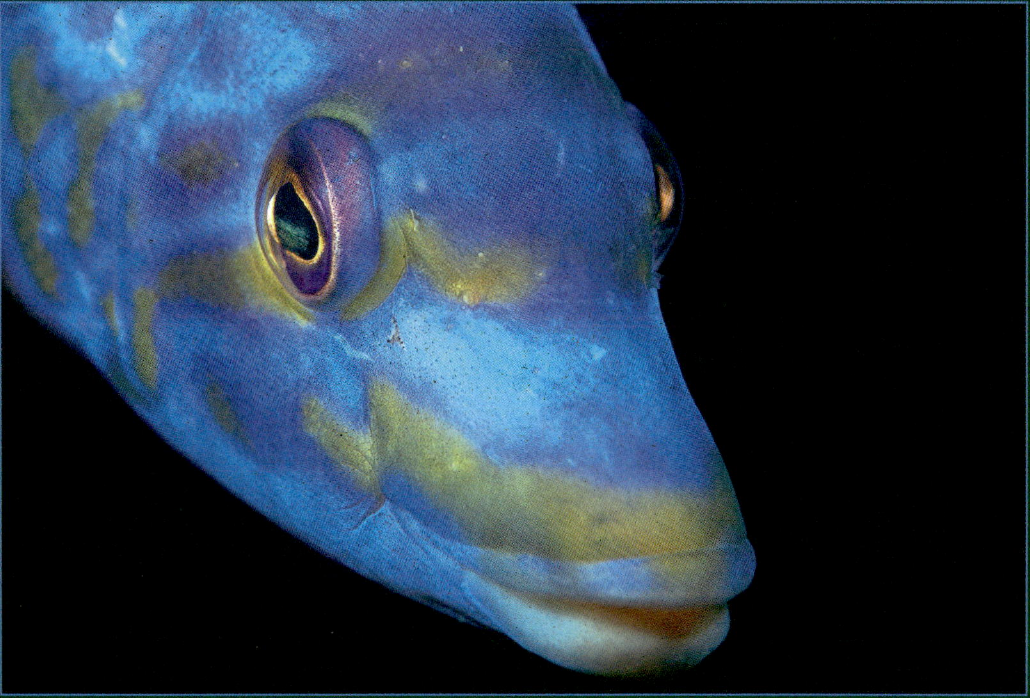

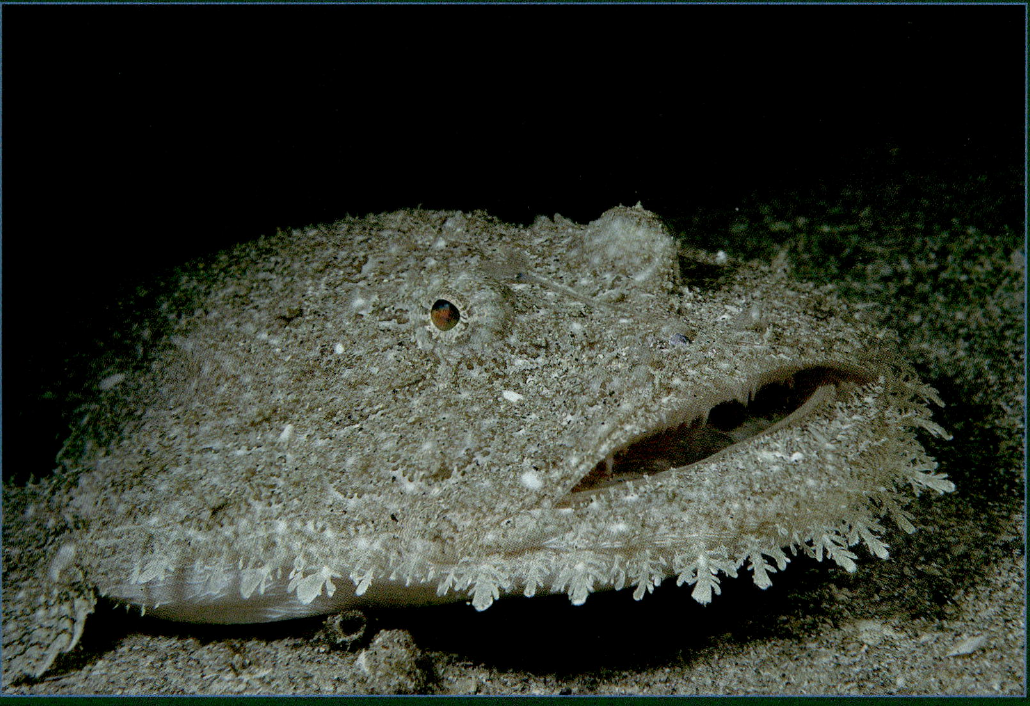

Cuckoo wrasse (top), and monkfish or angler fish

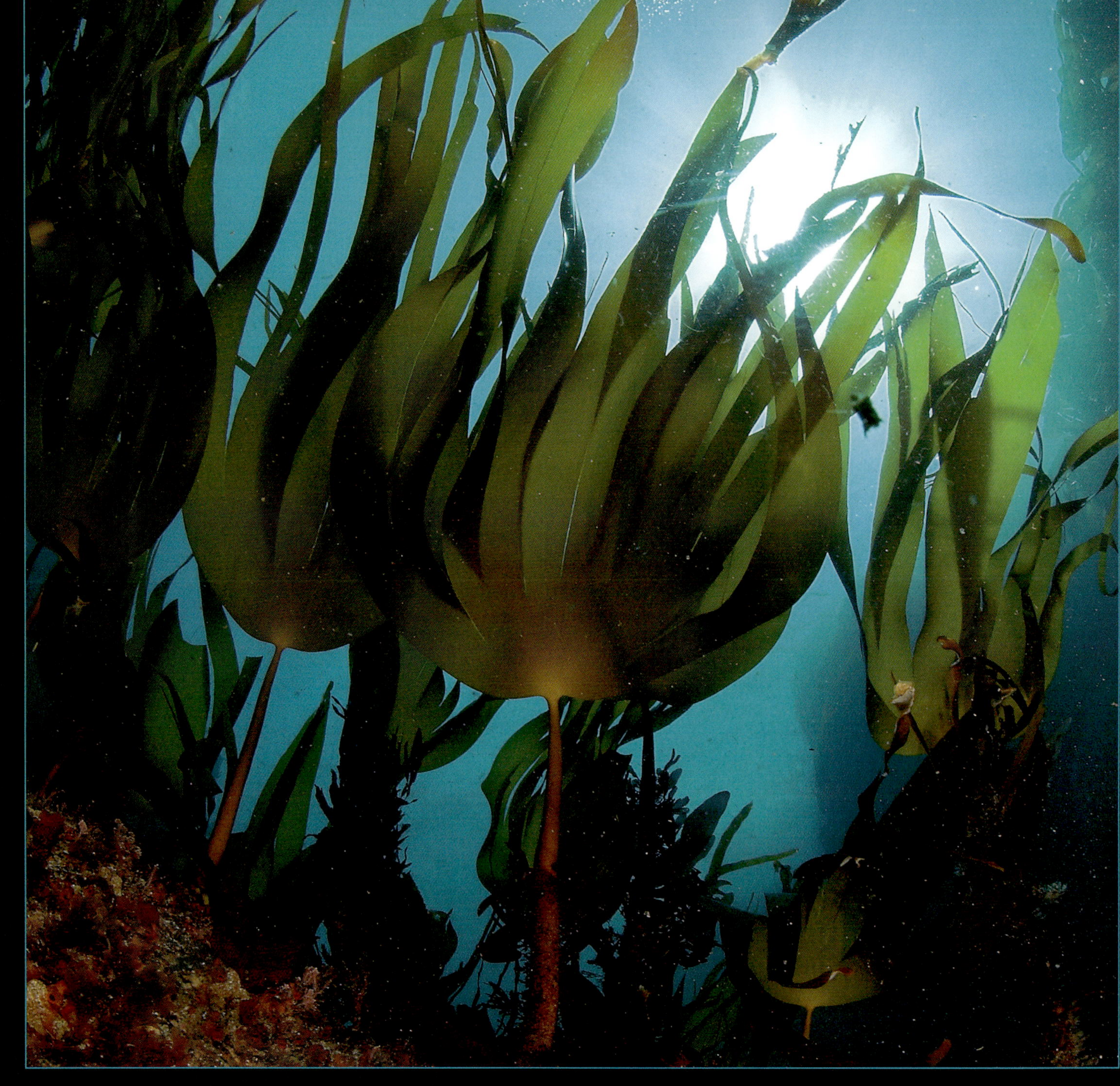

Kelp fronds on reef top

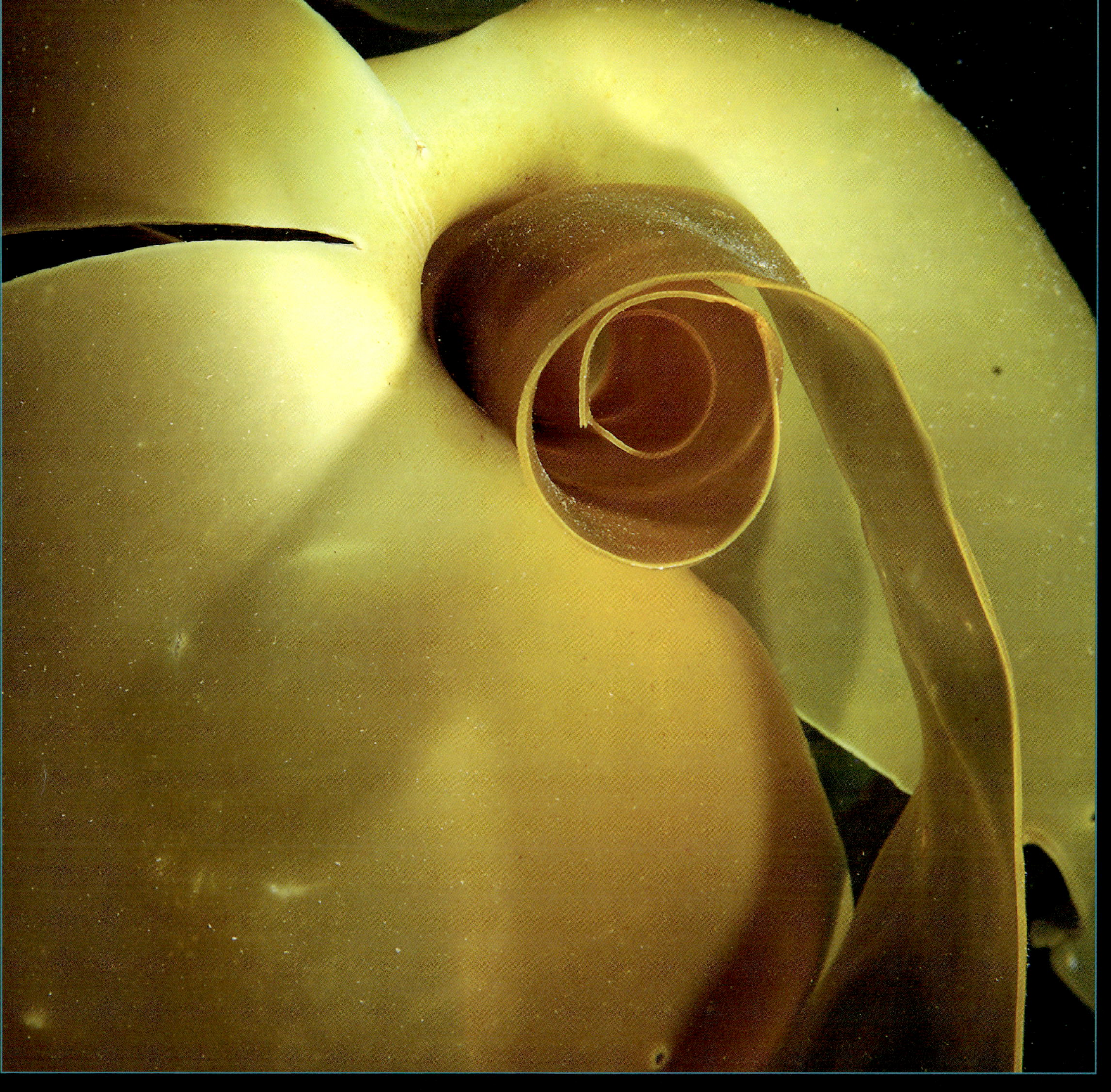

Natural patterns in kelp fronds

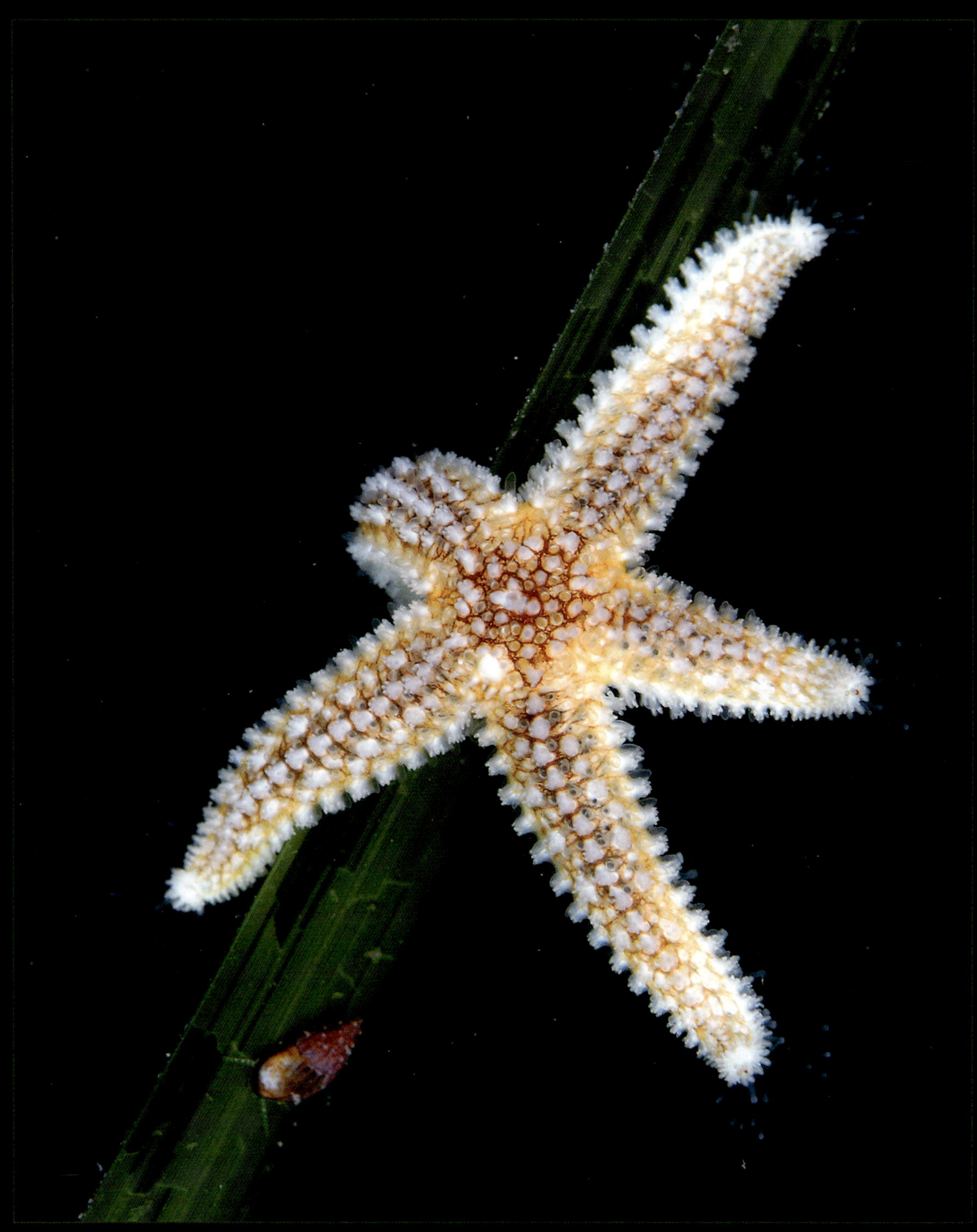

Juvenile common starfish on eelgrass

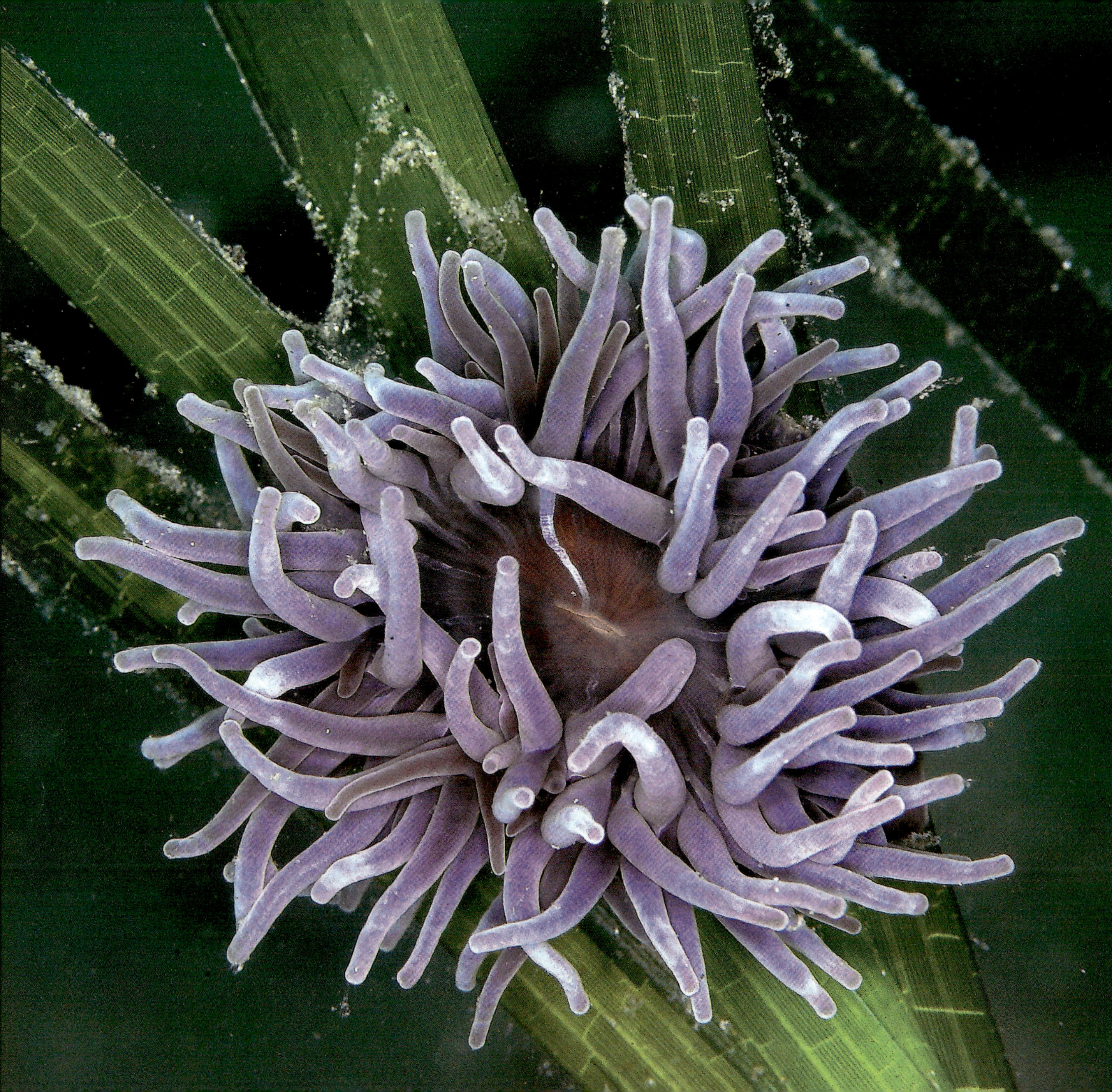

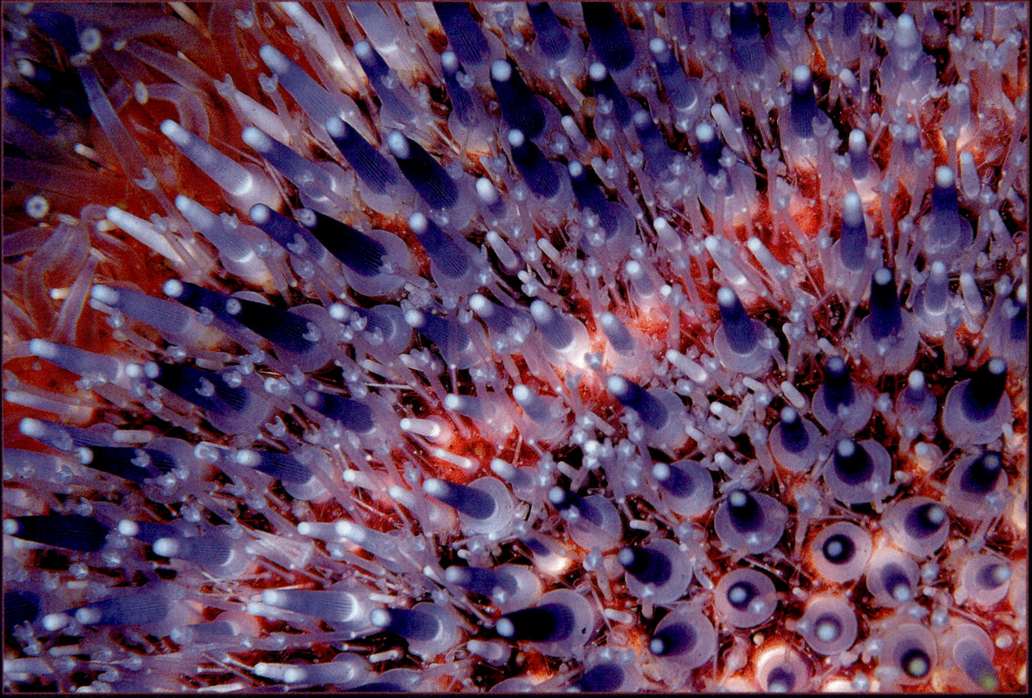

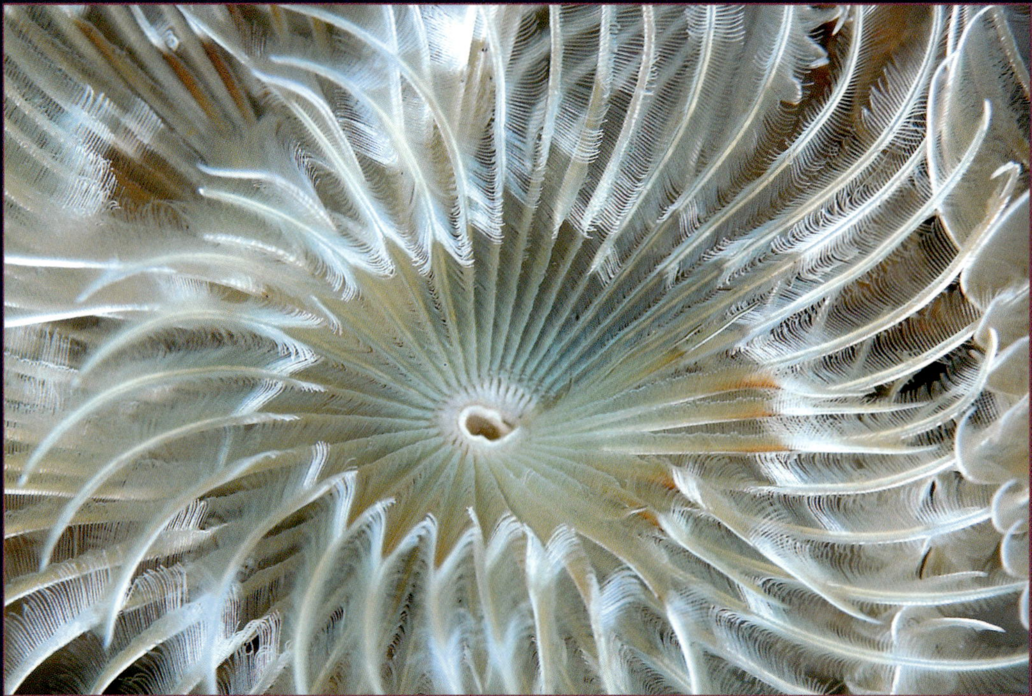

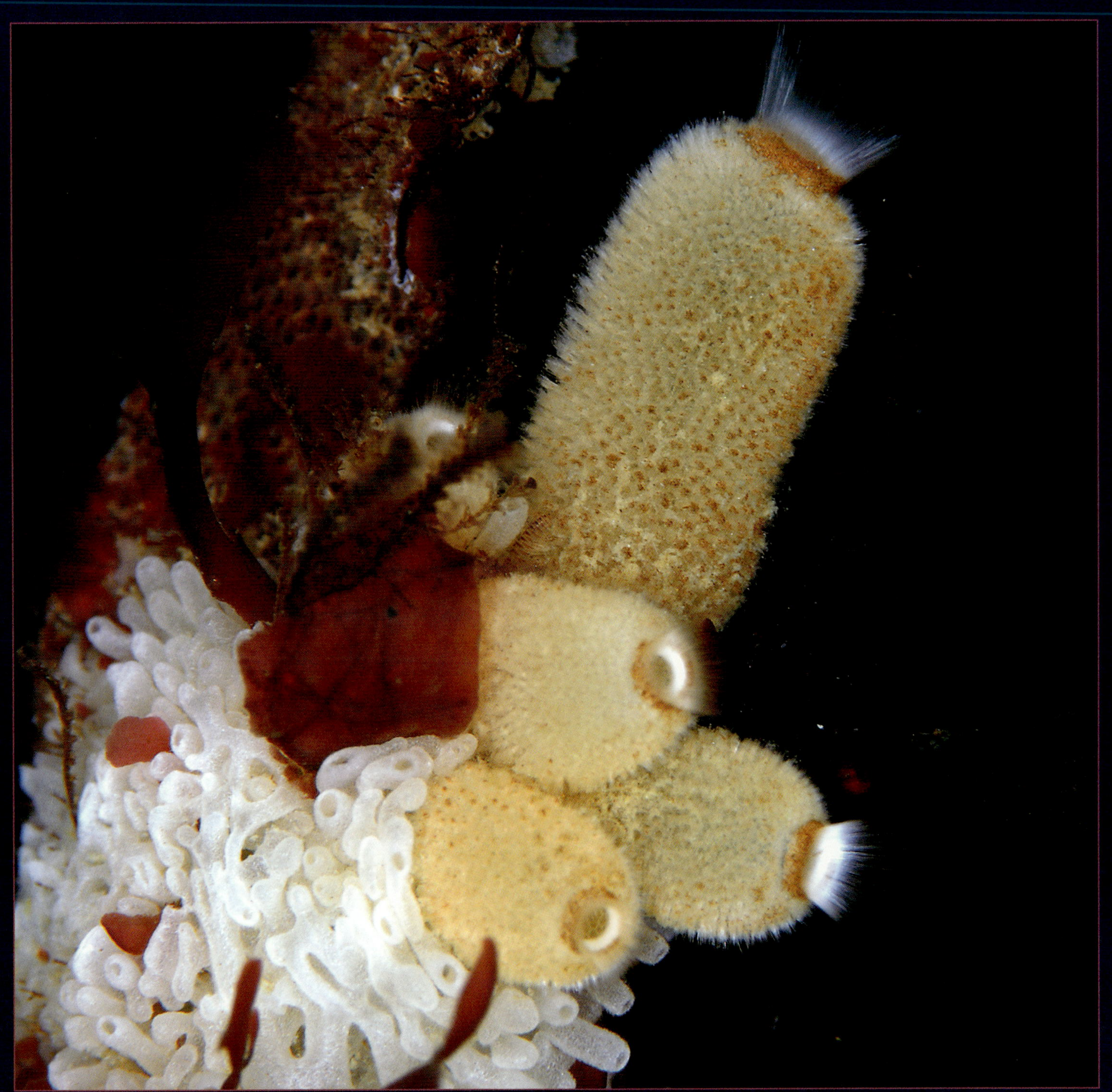

Sea squirt colony on kelp stype

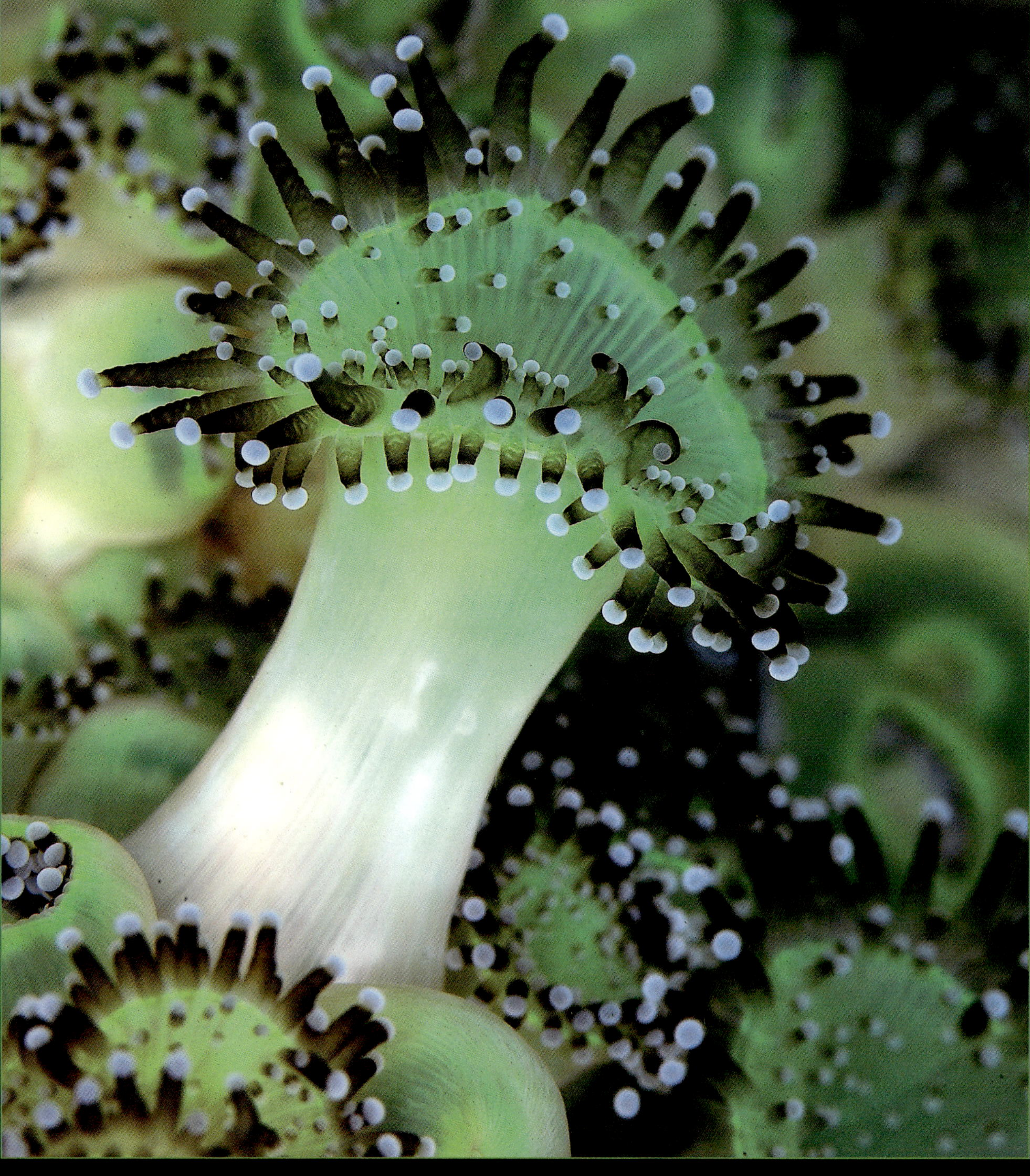

Jewel anemones

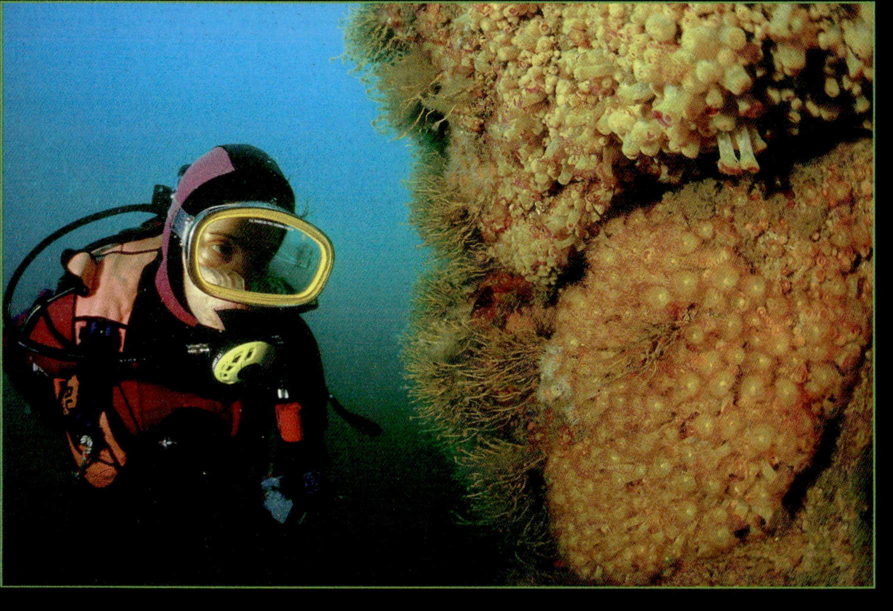

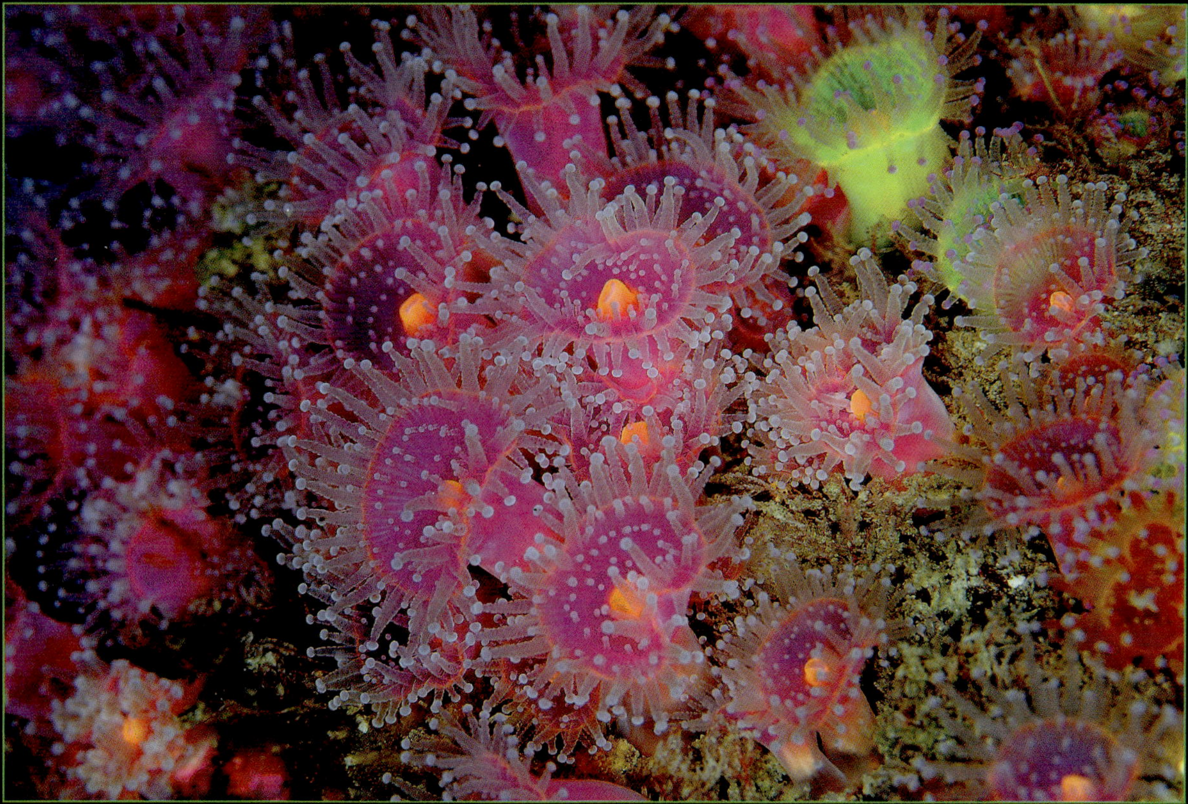

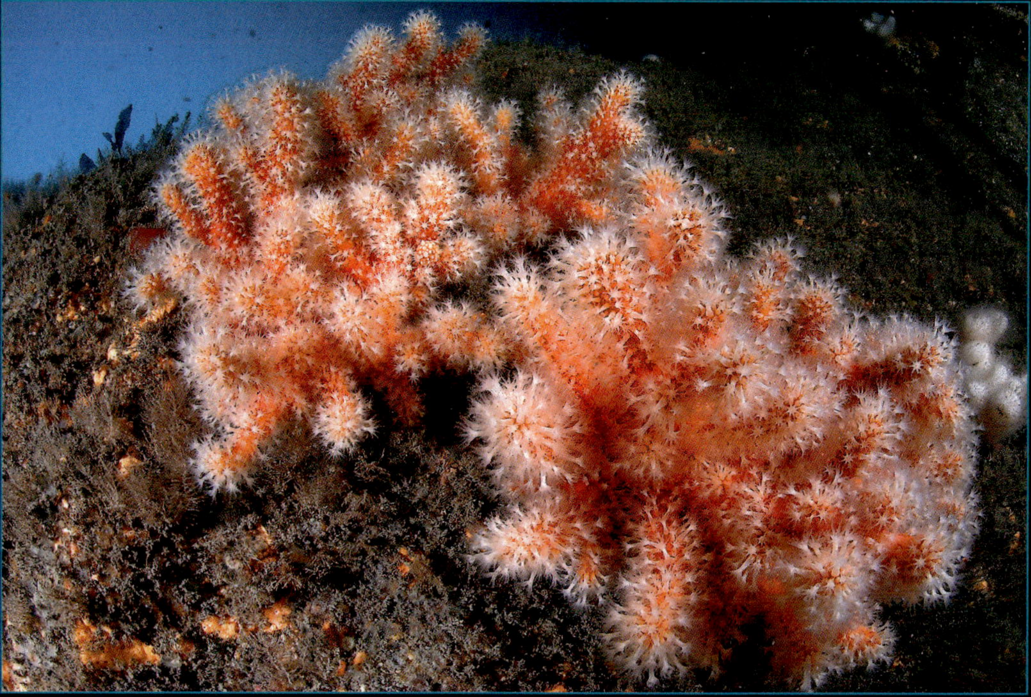

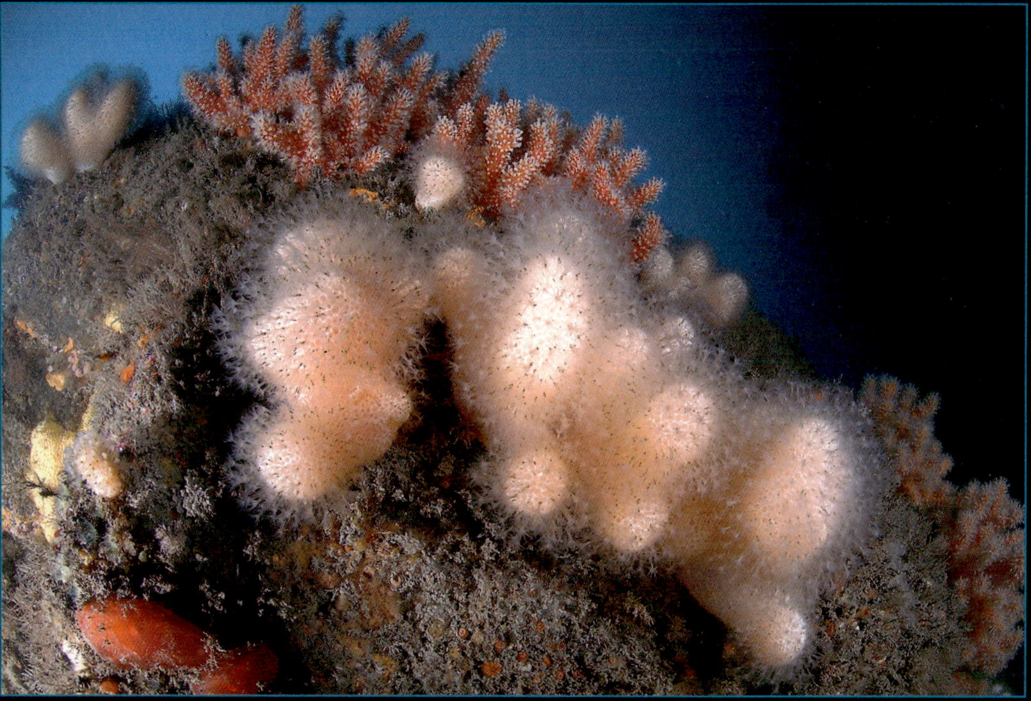

Red (top) and white soft corals (dead men’s fingers)

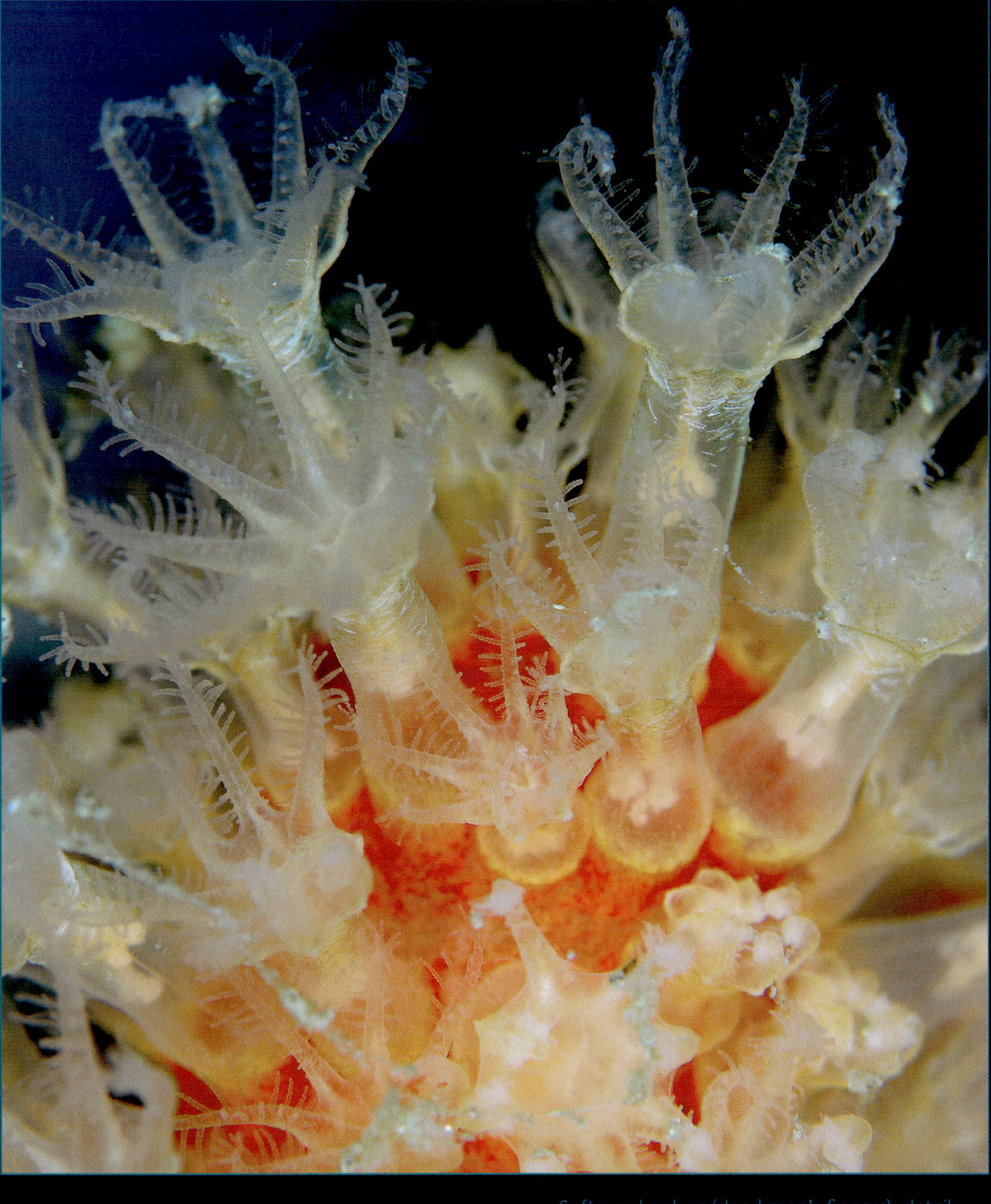

Soft coral polyps (dead men's fingers), detail

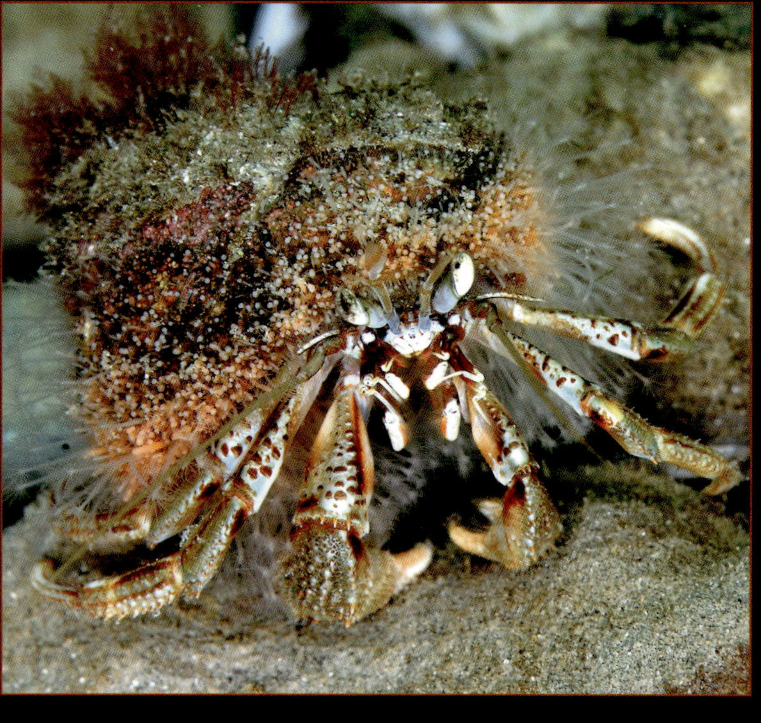

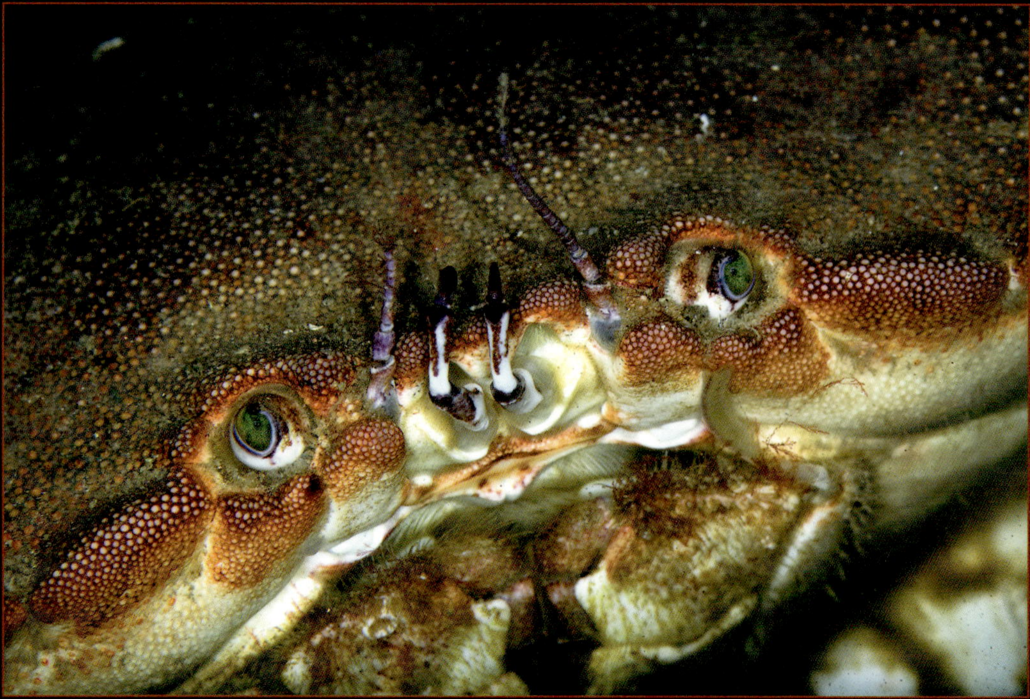

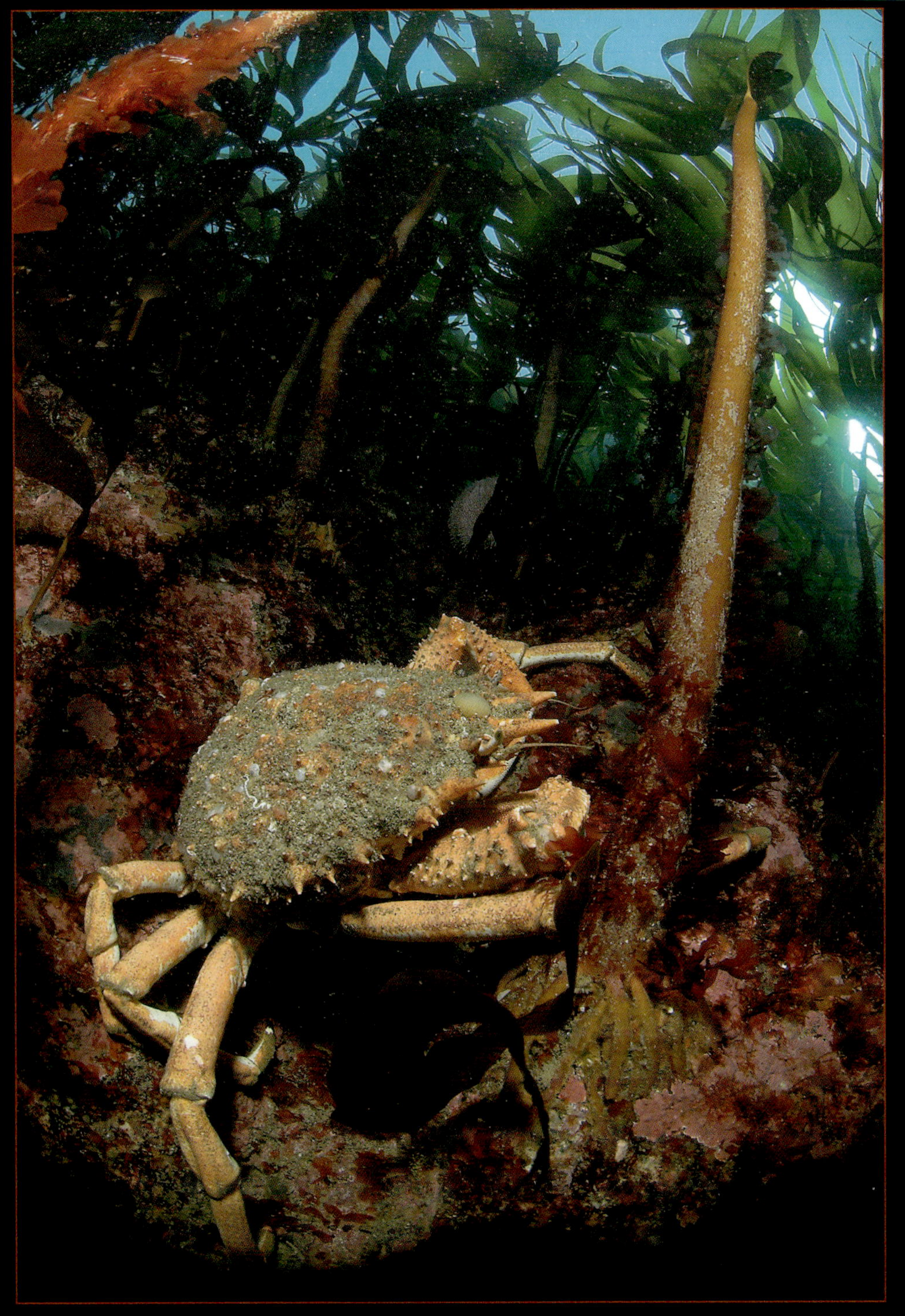

Spider crab

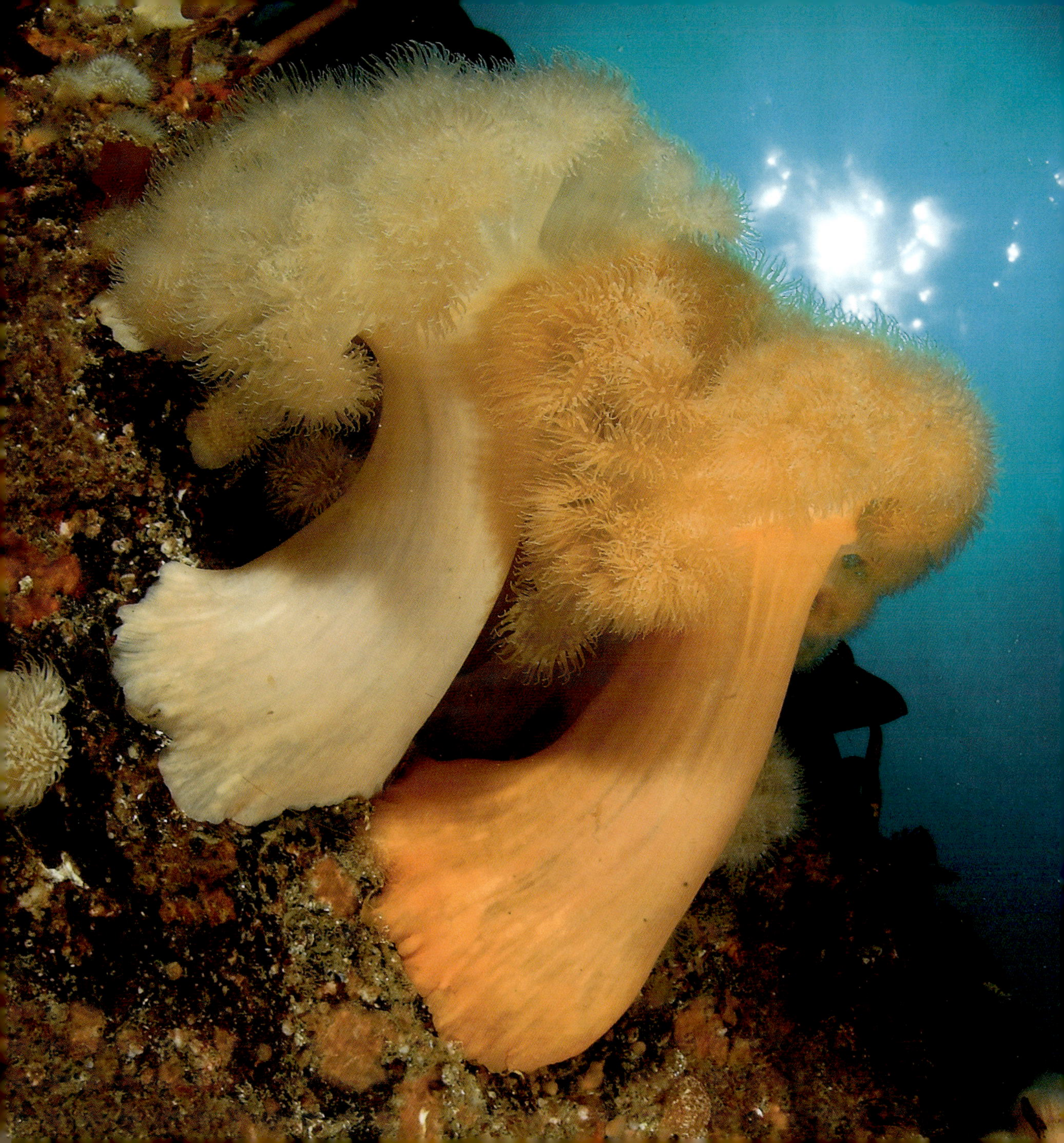

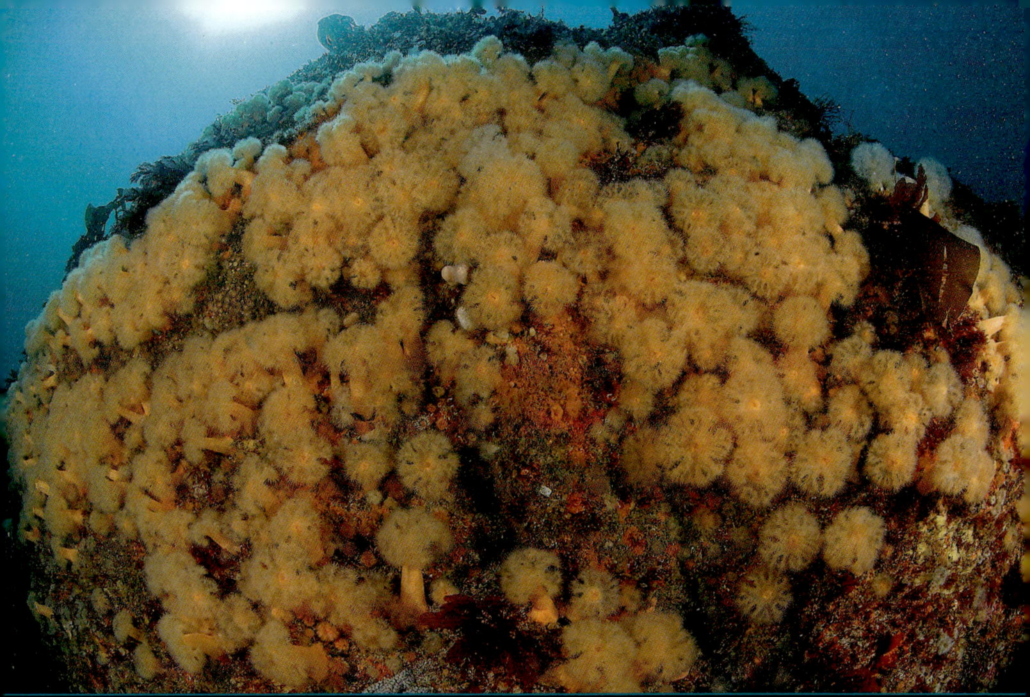

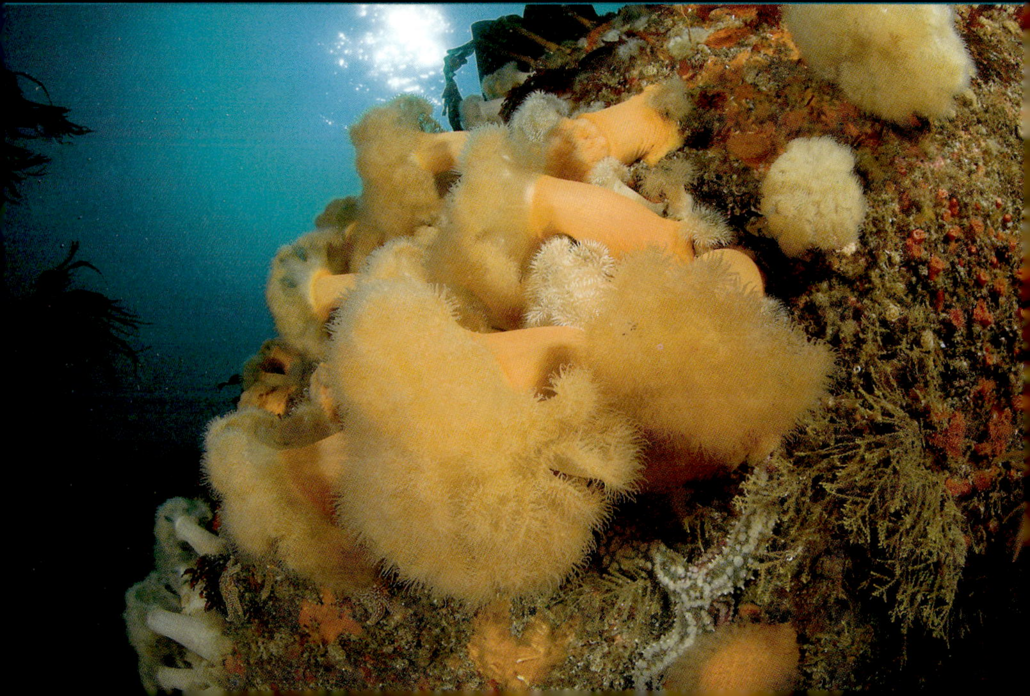

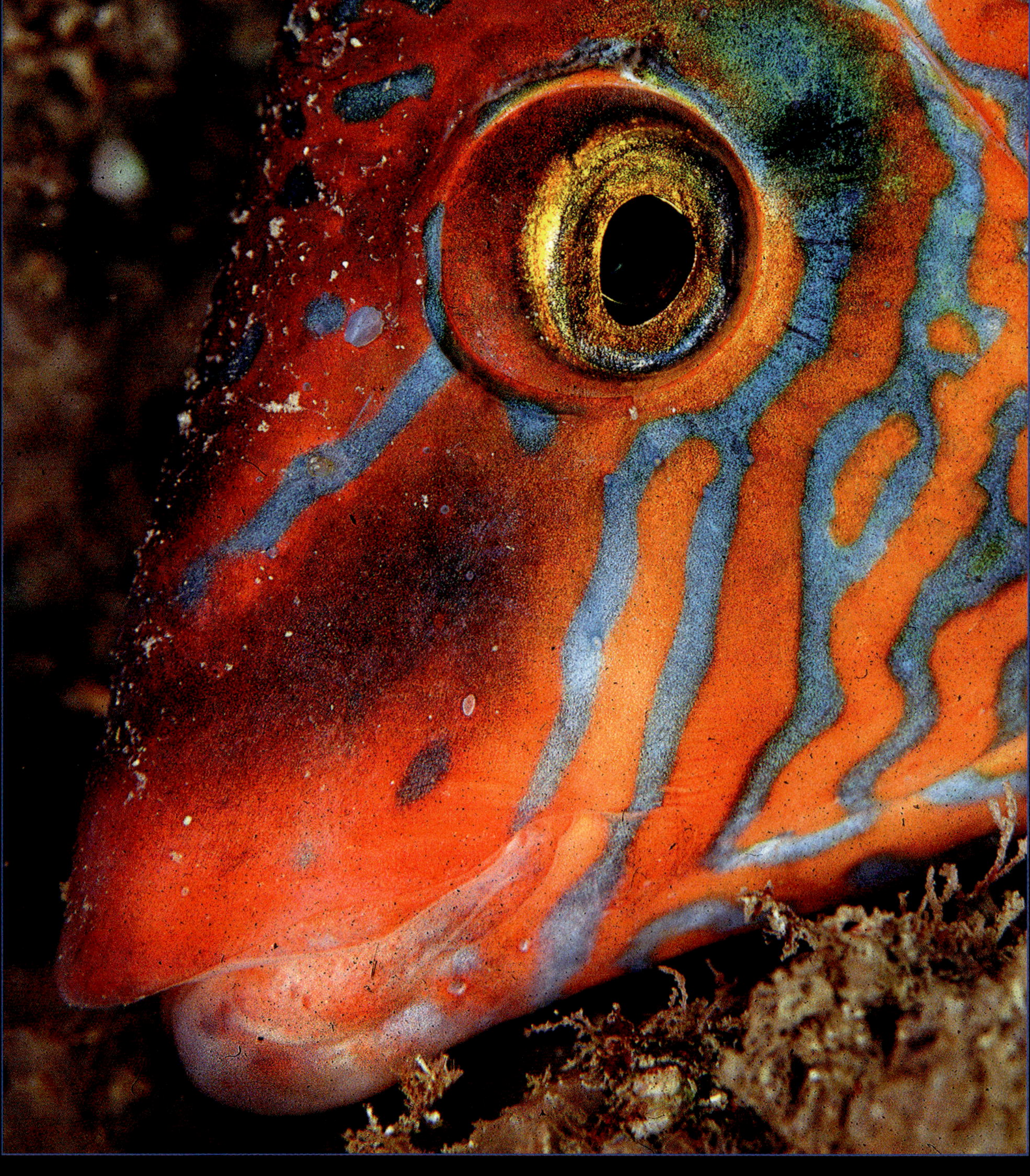

Corkwing wrasse

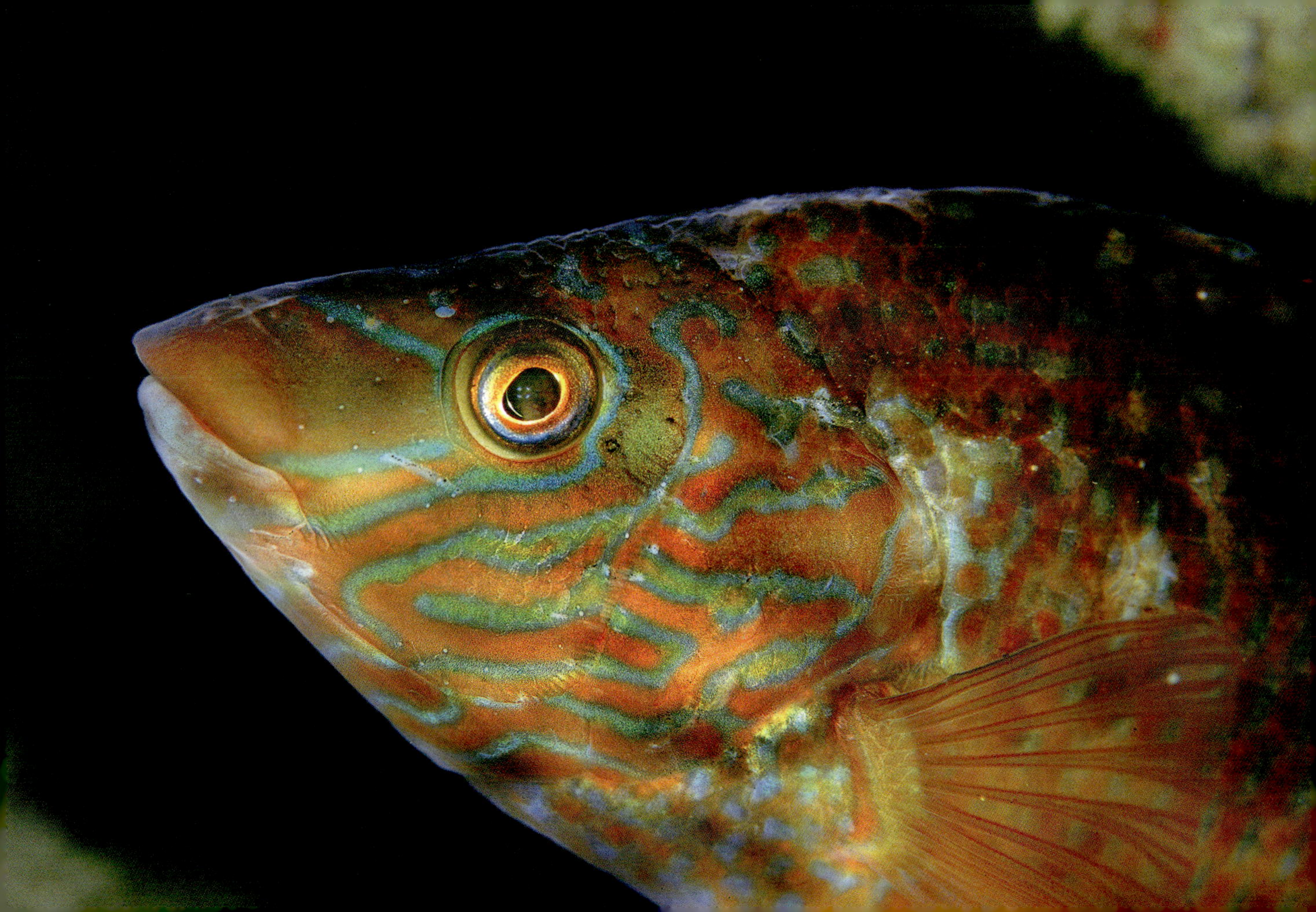

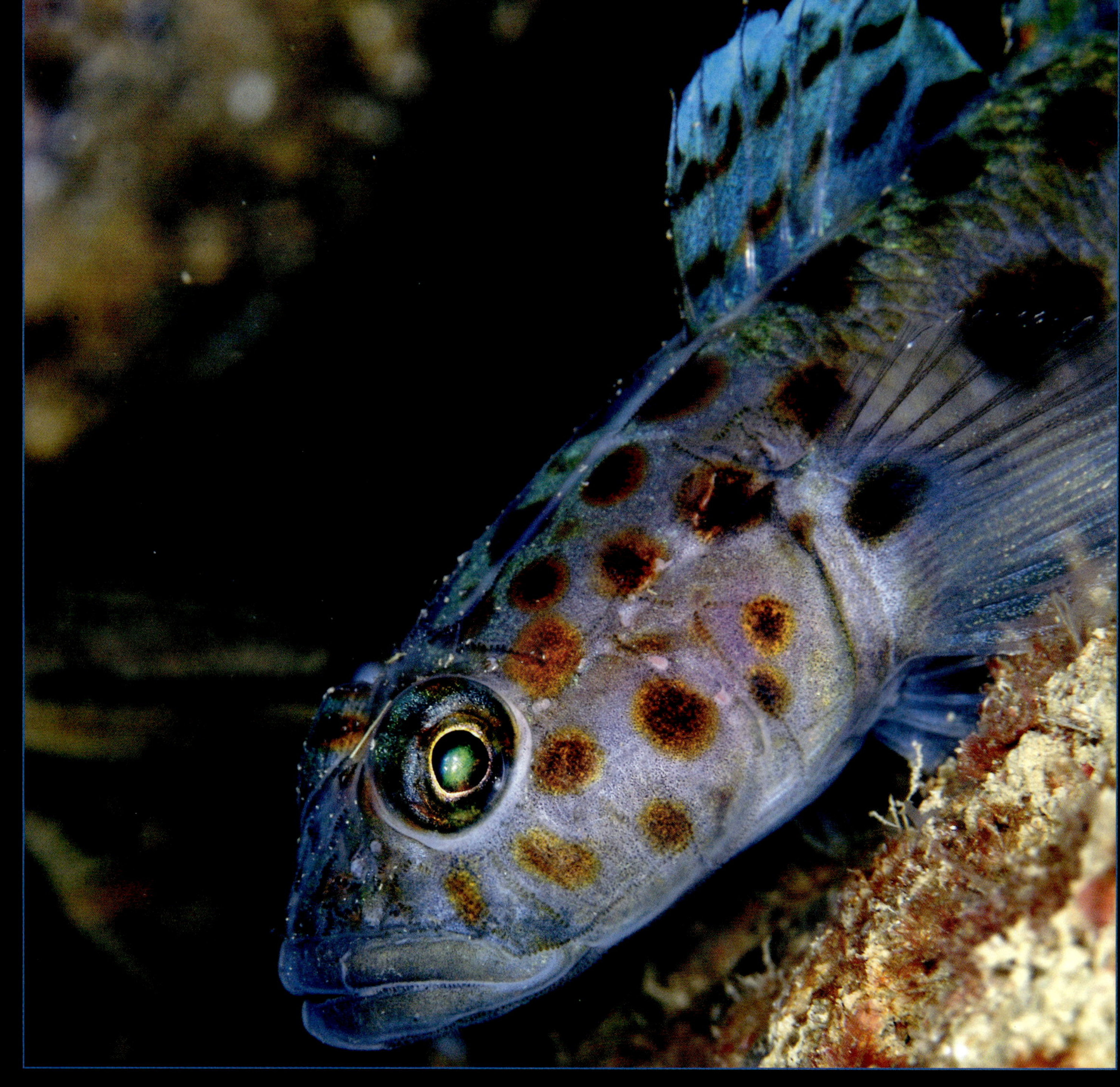

Leopard-spotted goby

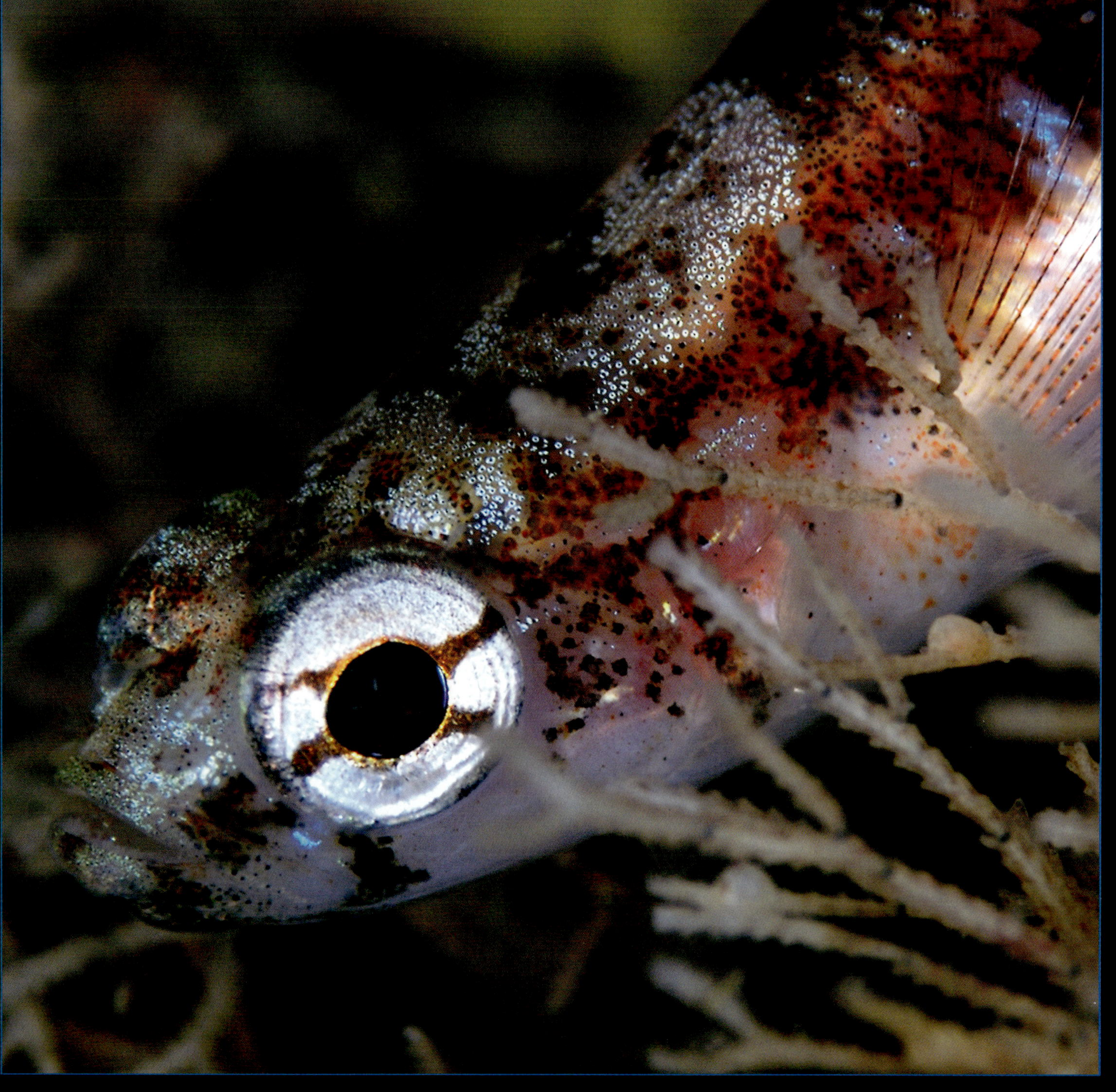

Two-spot goby

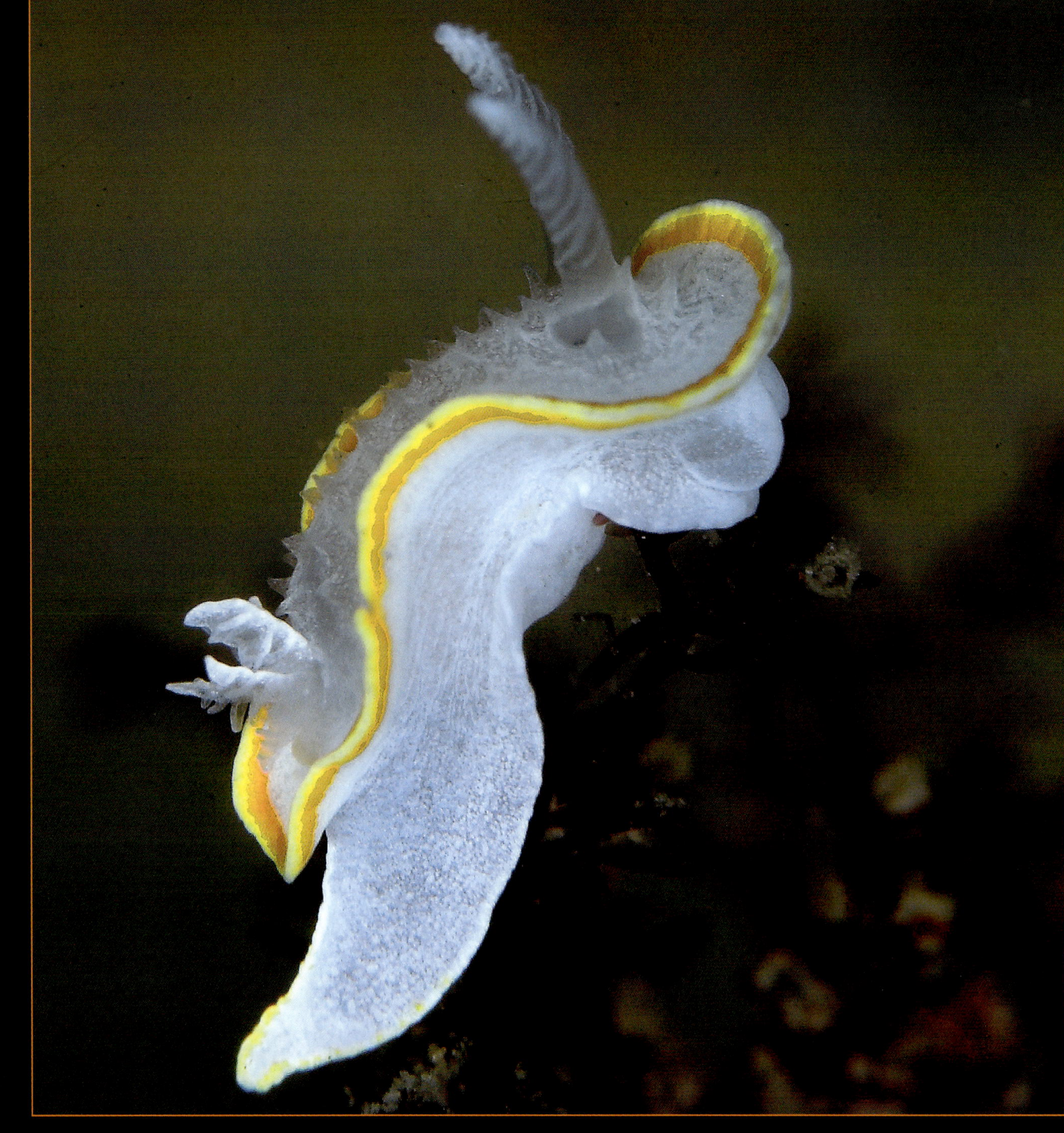

Sea slug, *Diaphorodoris luteocincta*

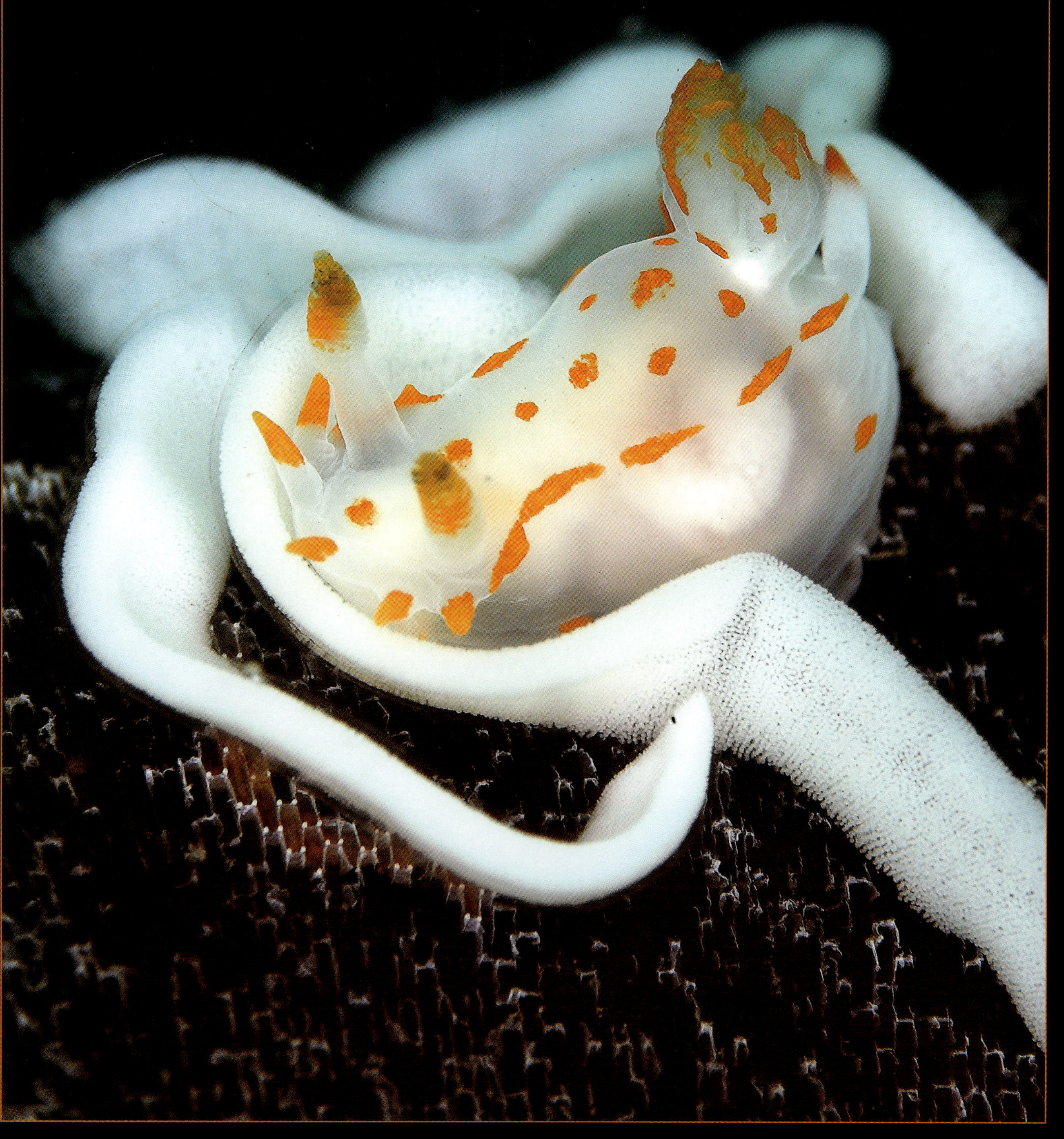

Sea slug, *Polycera quadrilineata* laying eggs on kelp

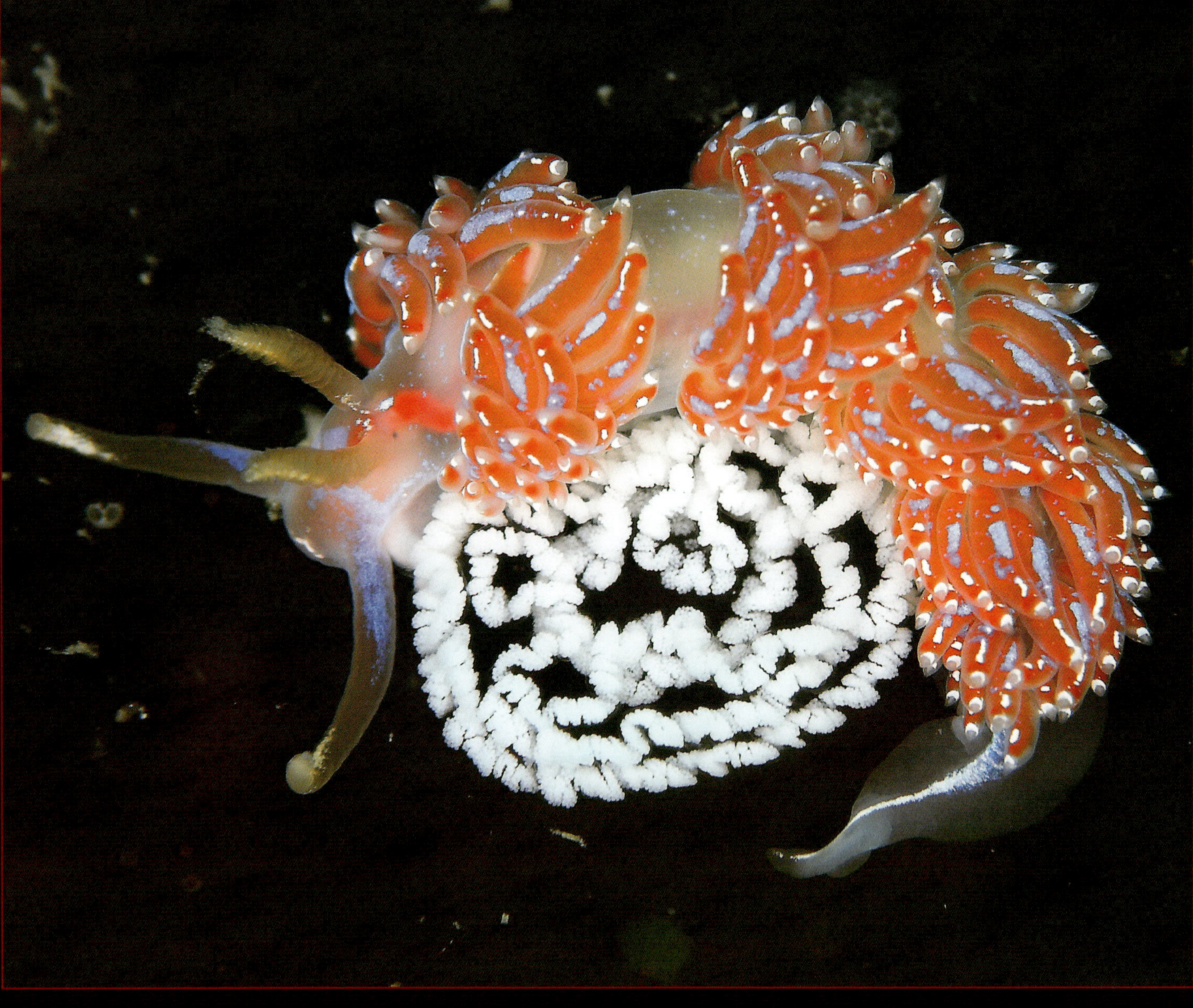

Sea slug, *Coryphella browni*, laying eggs on kelp

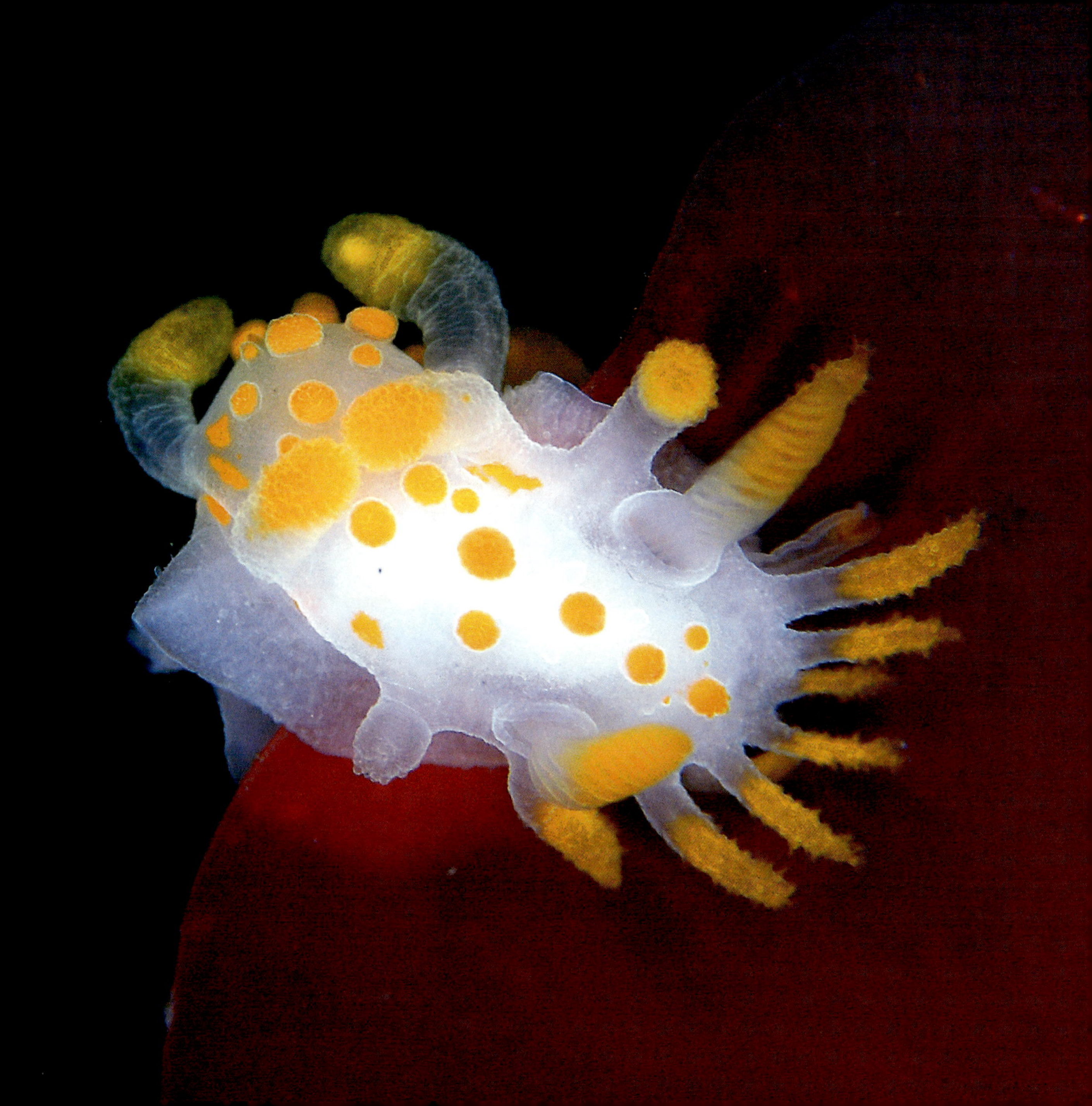

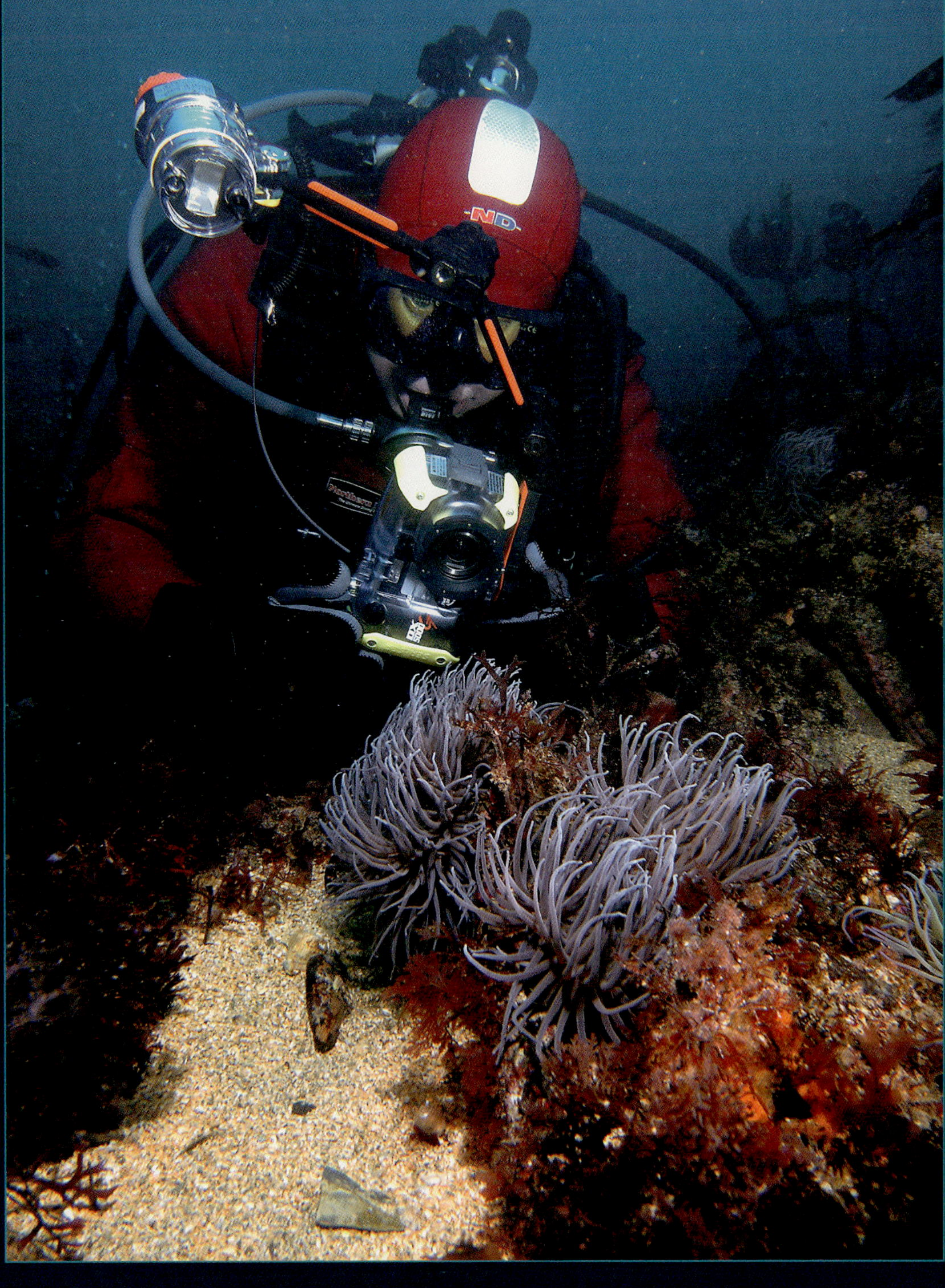

Diver photographing snakelocks anemones

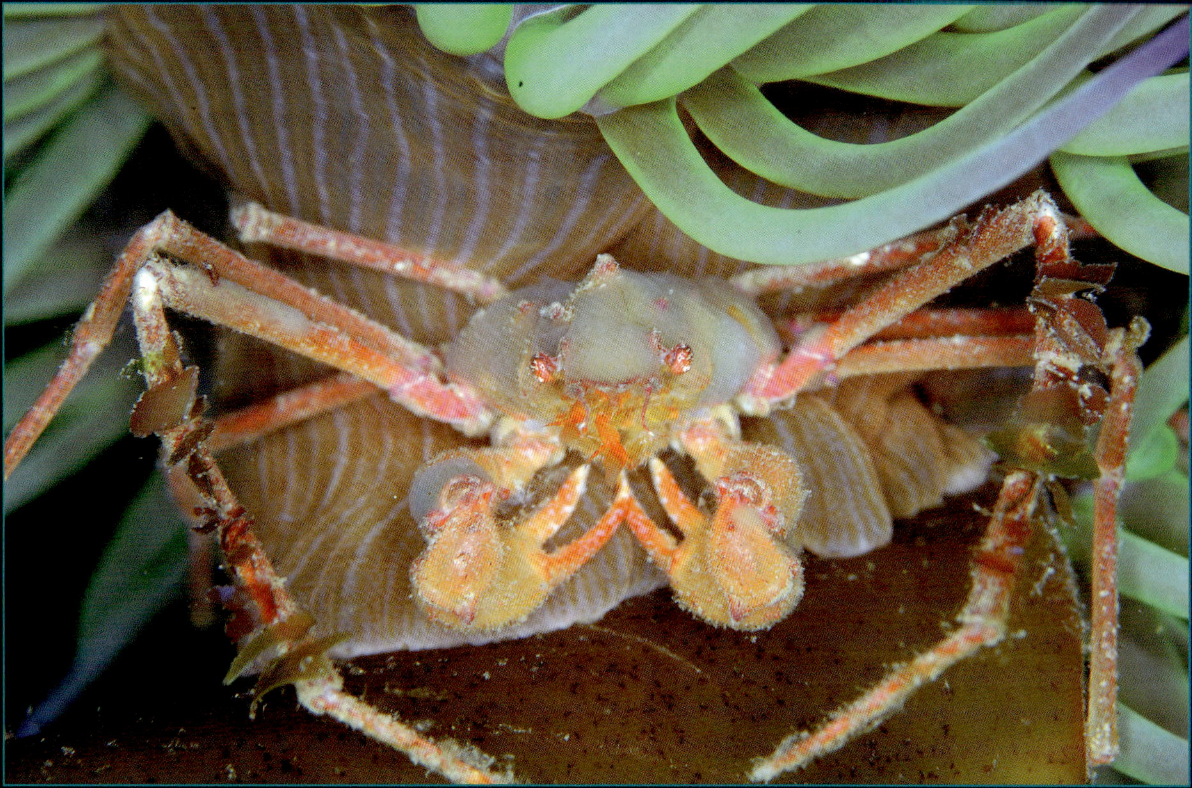

Spider crab living on snakelocks anemone

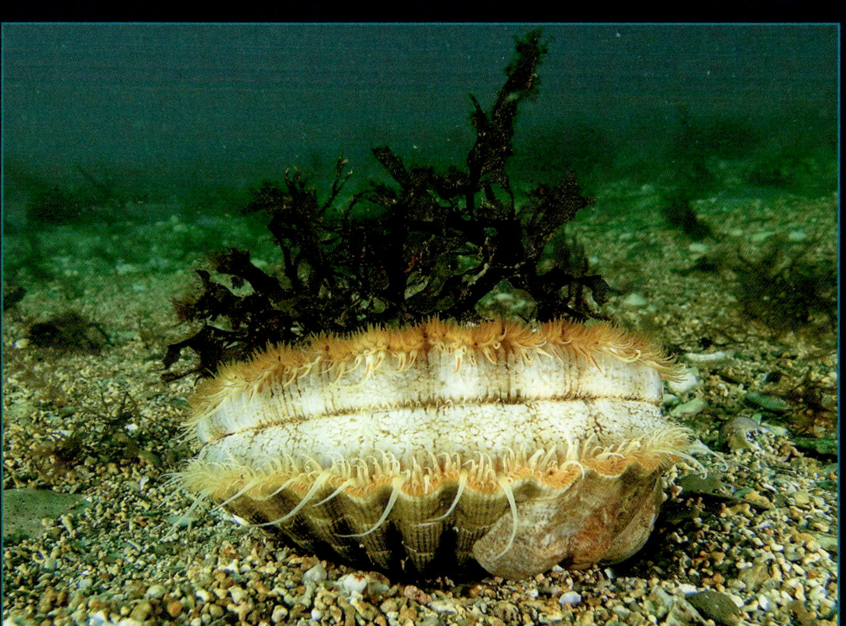

Scallop with seaweed decoration

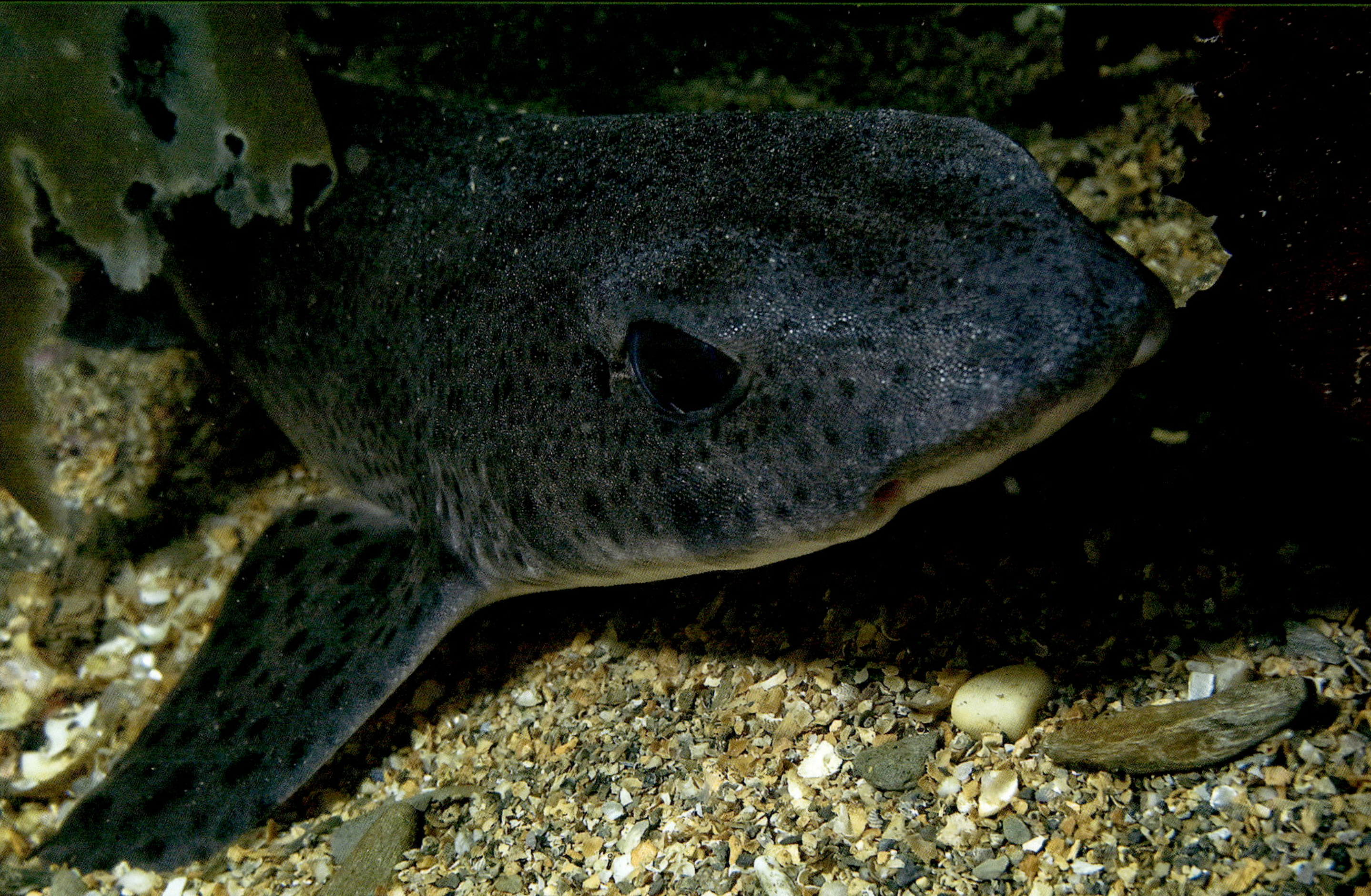

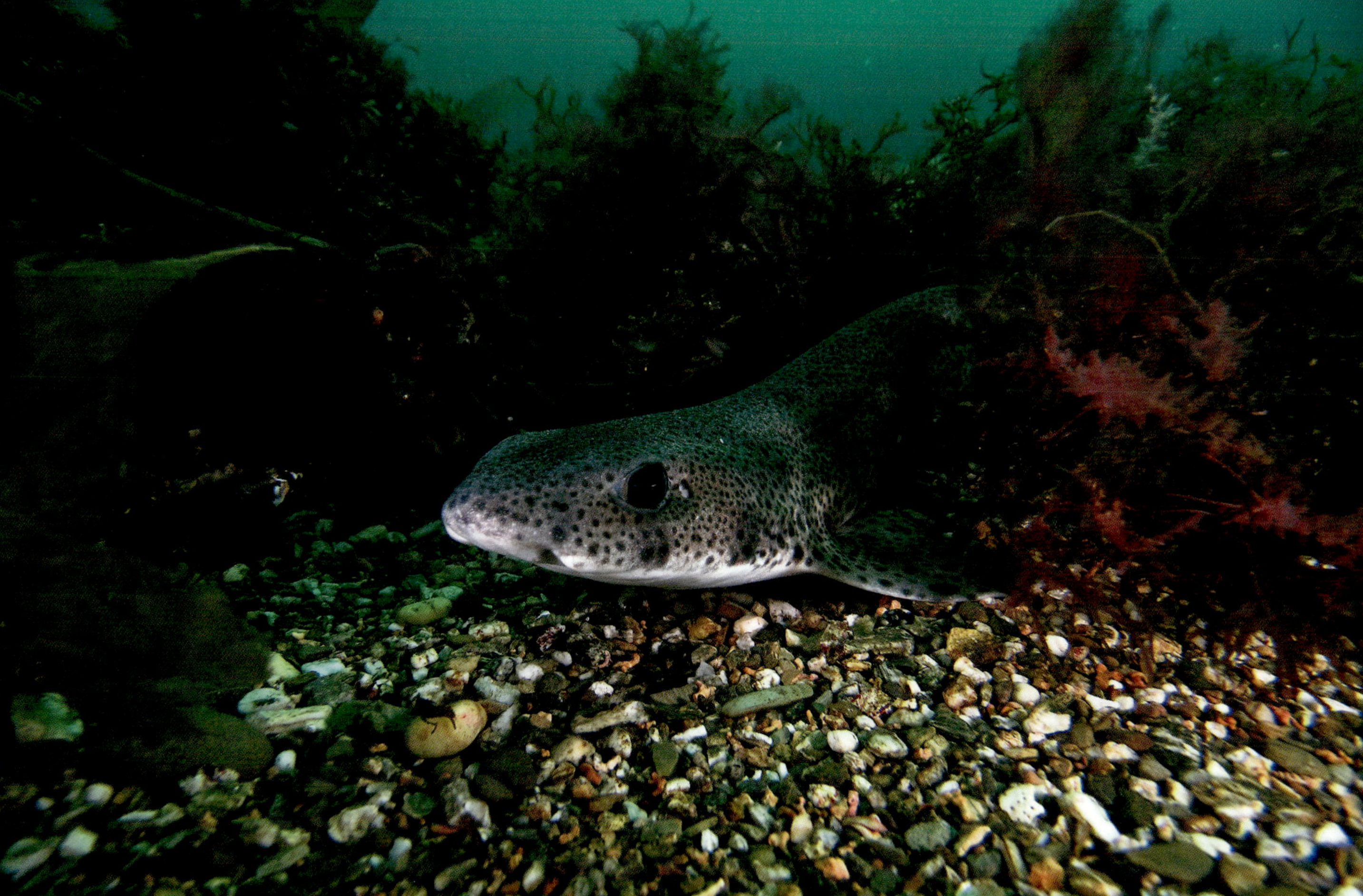

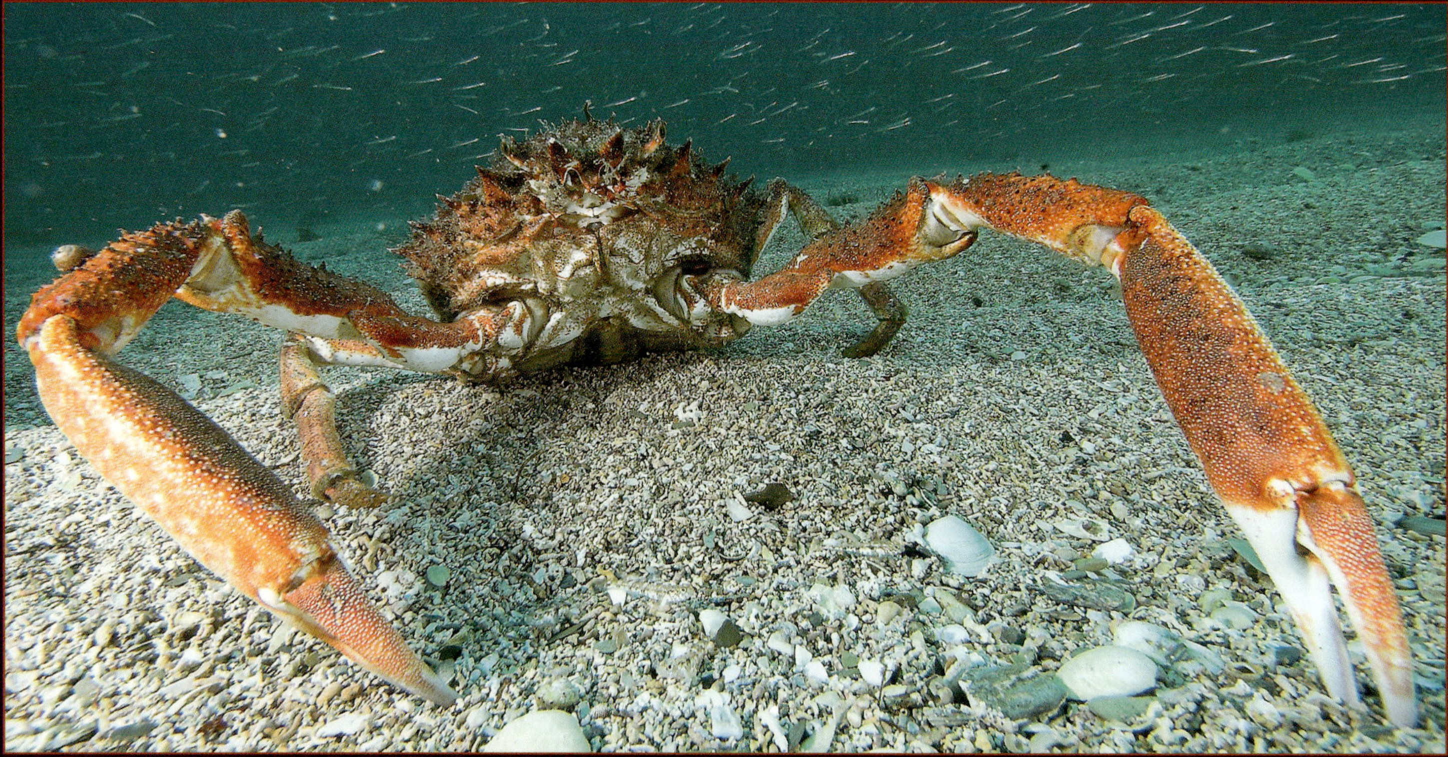

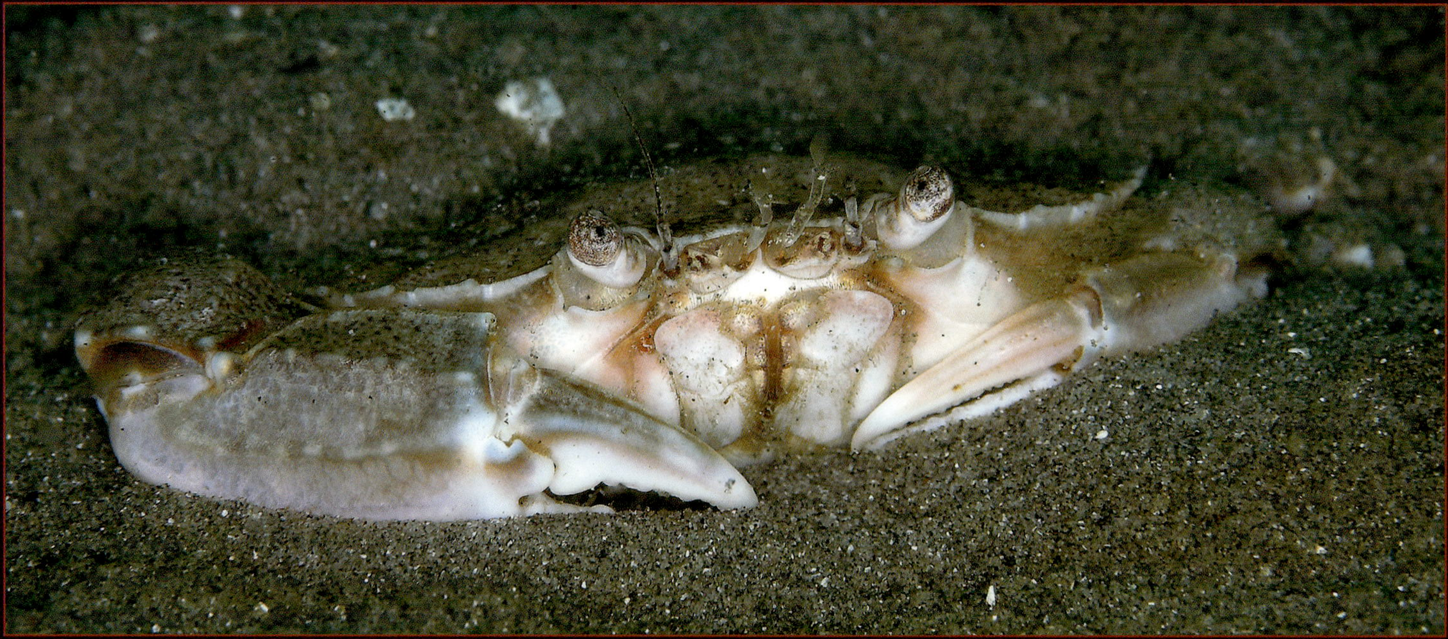

Spider crab (top), and shore crab

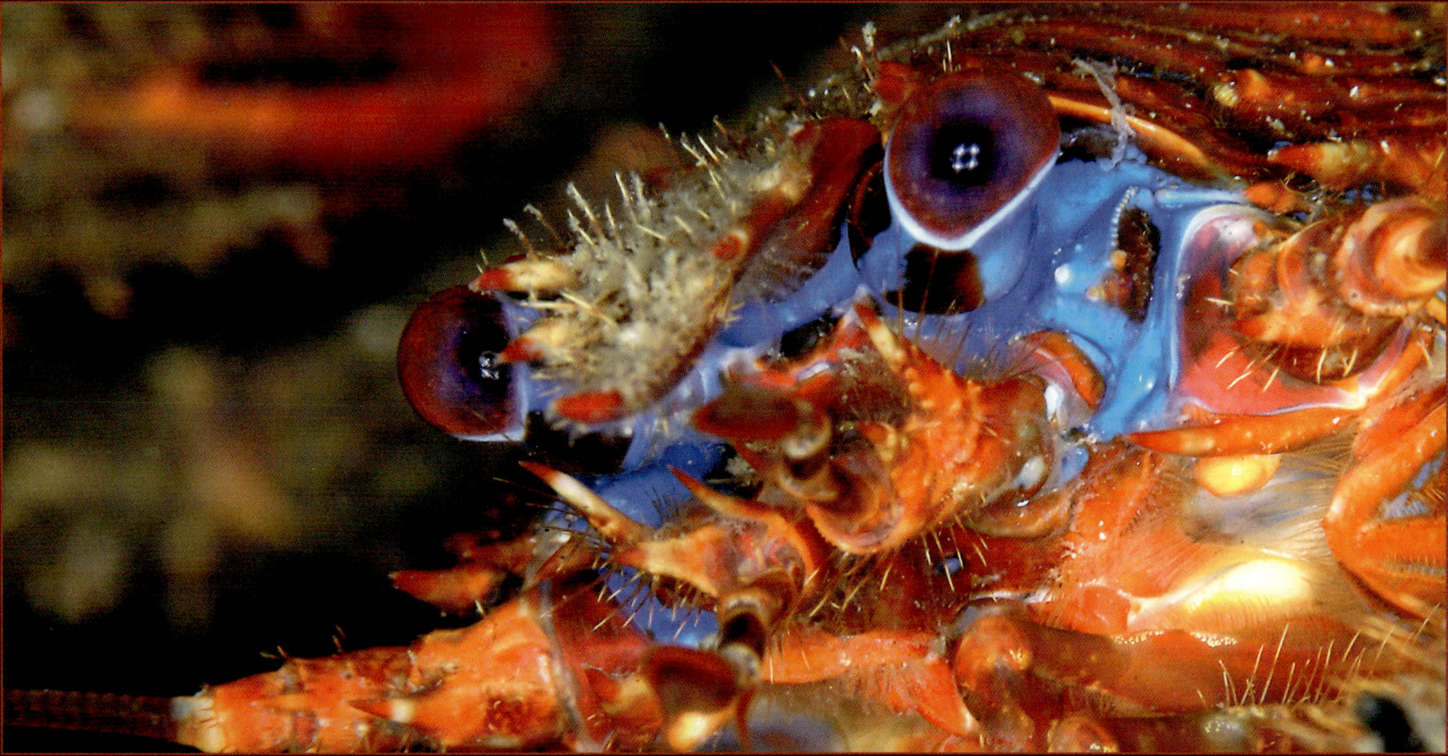

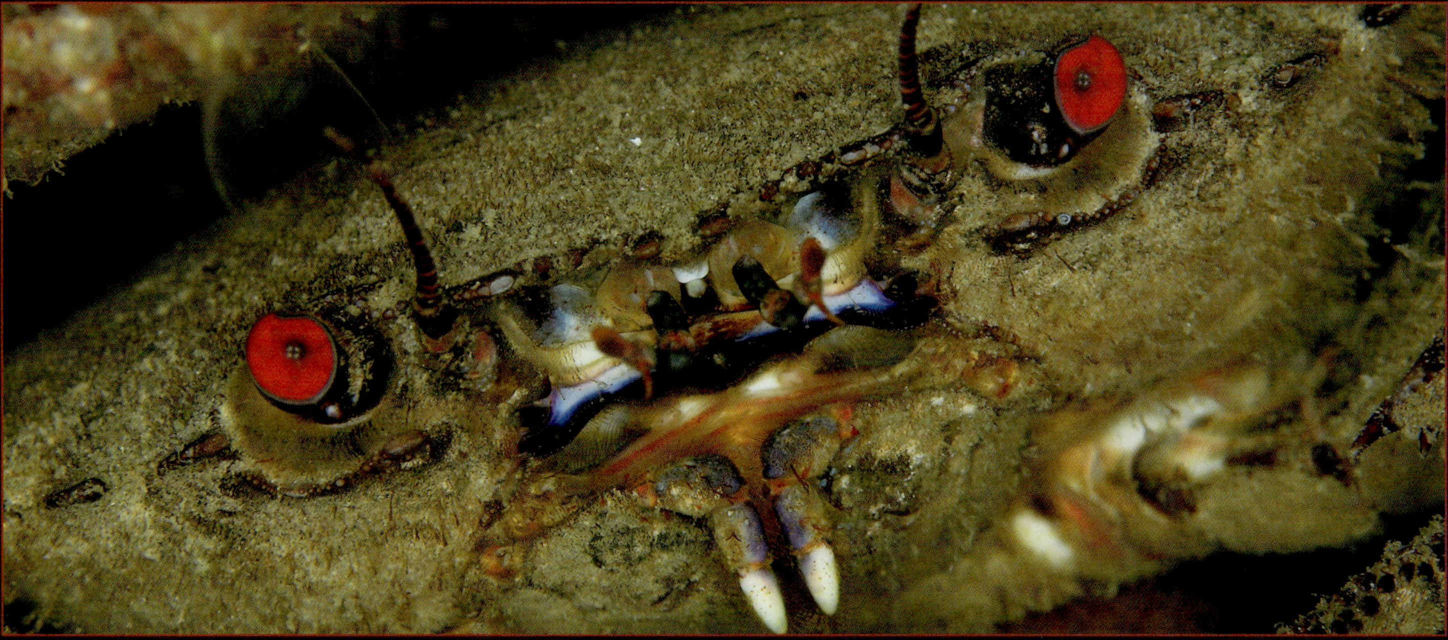

Squat lobster eyes (top), and velvet swimming crab

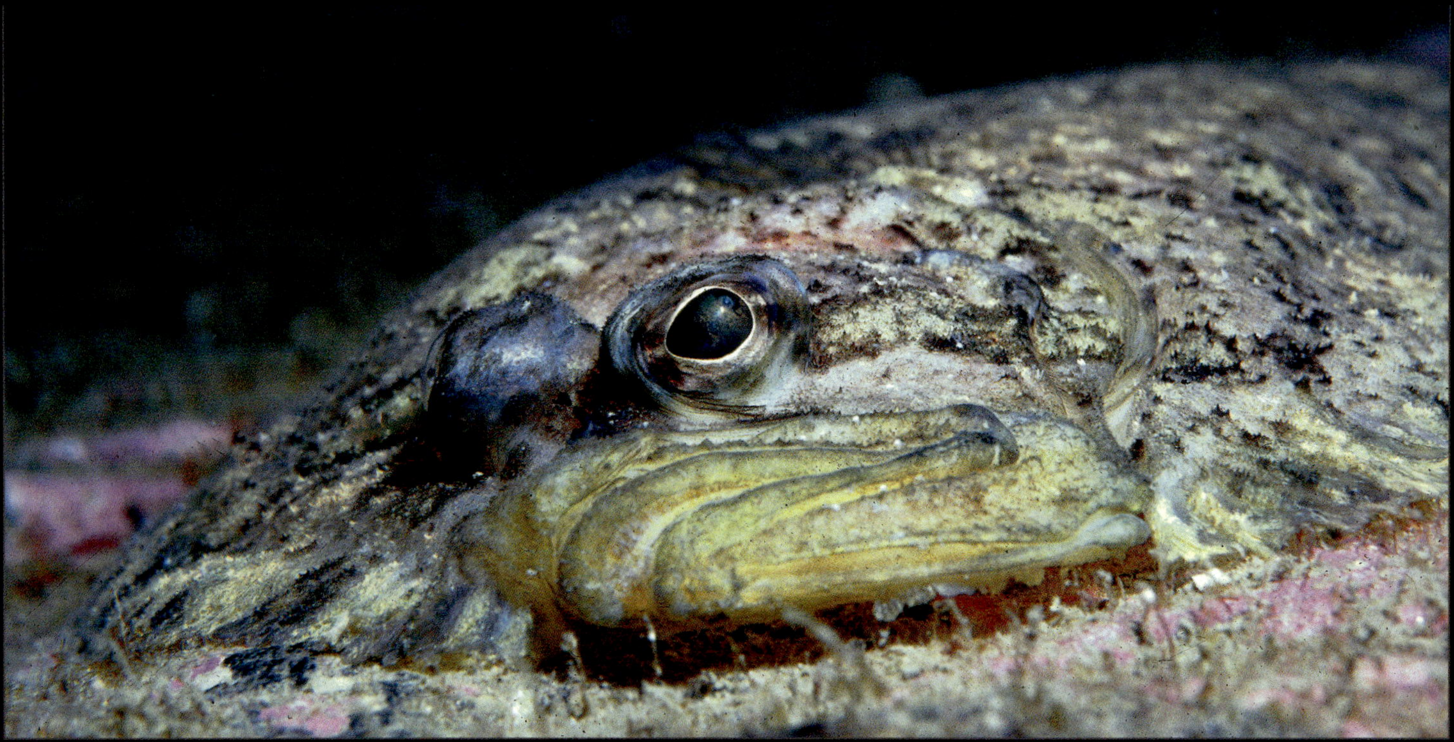

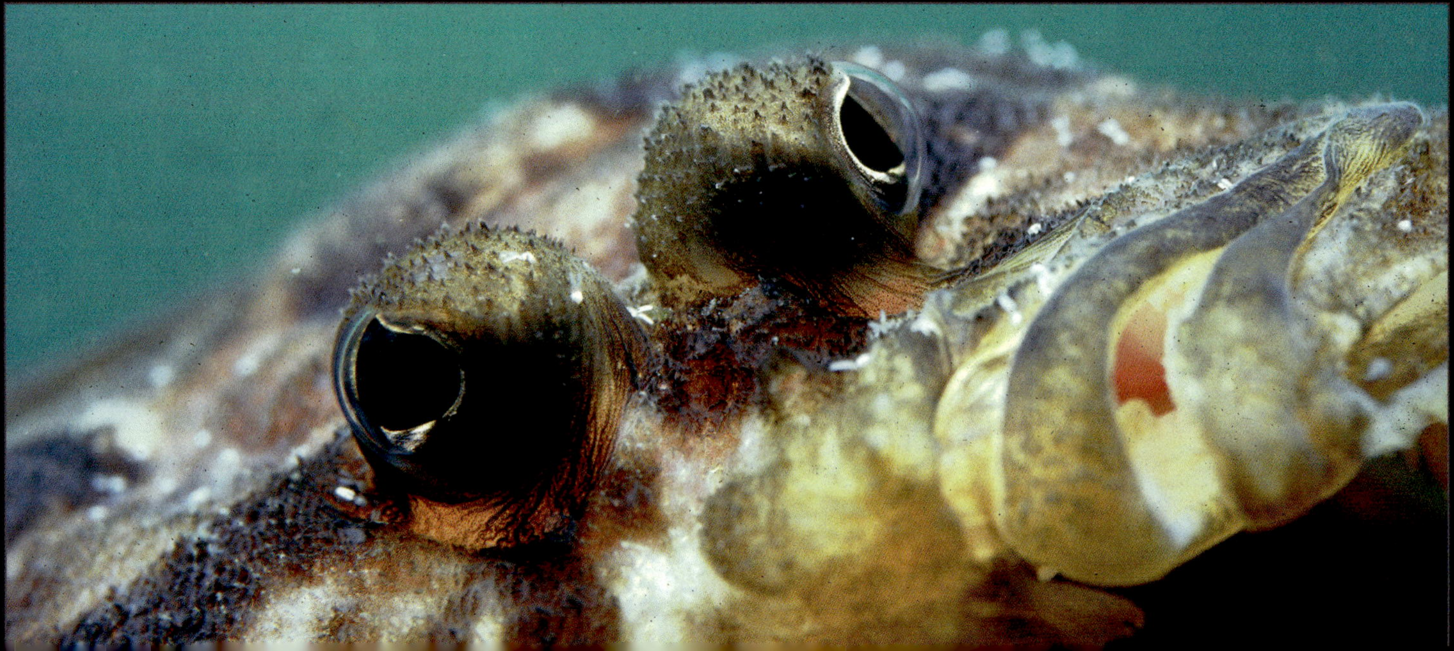

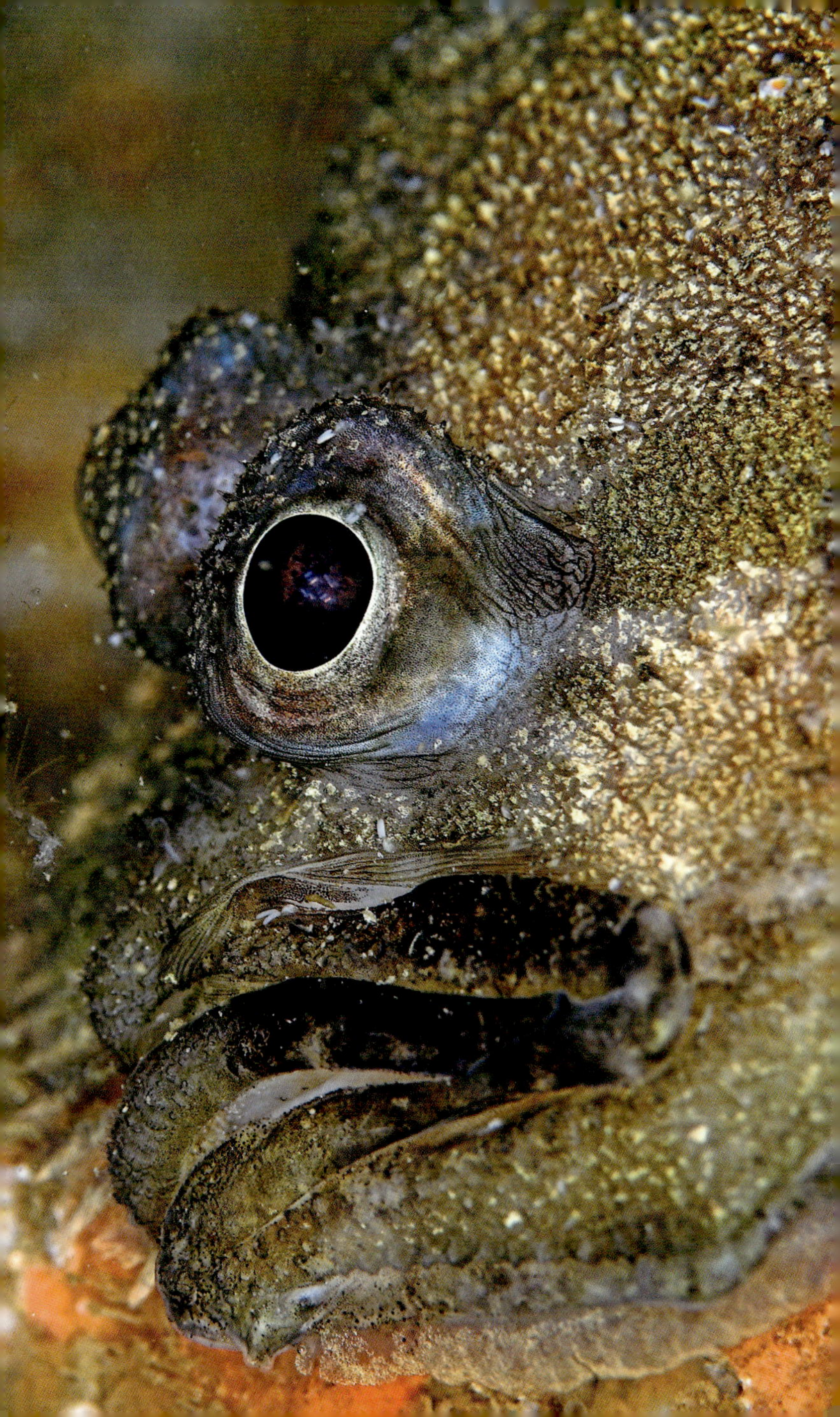

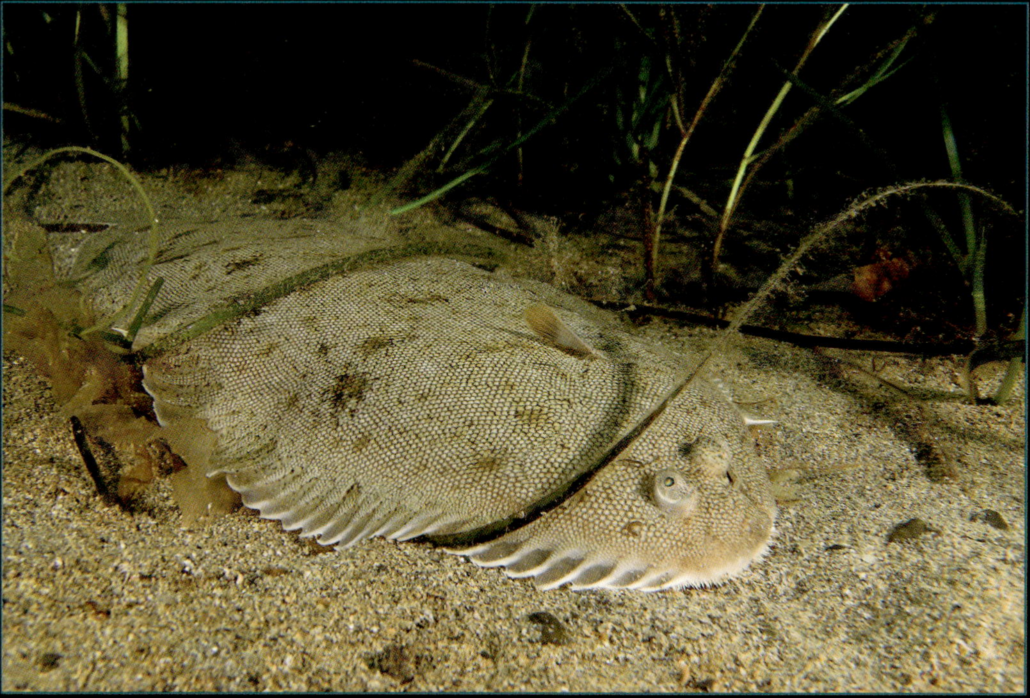

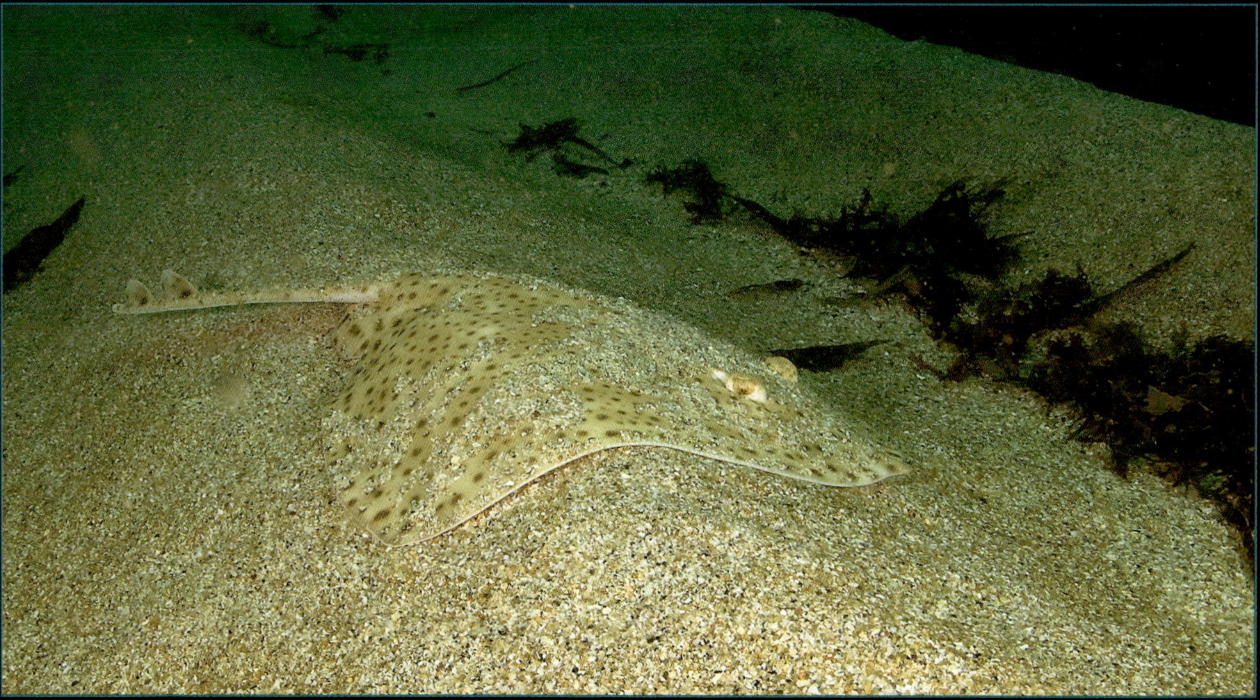

Dover sole (top), and thornback ray

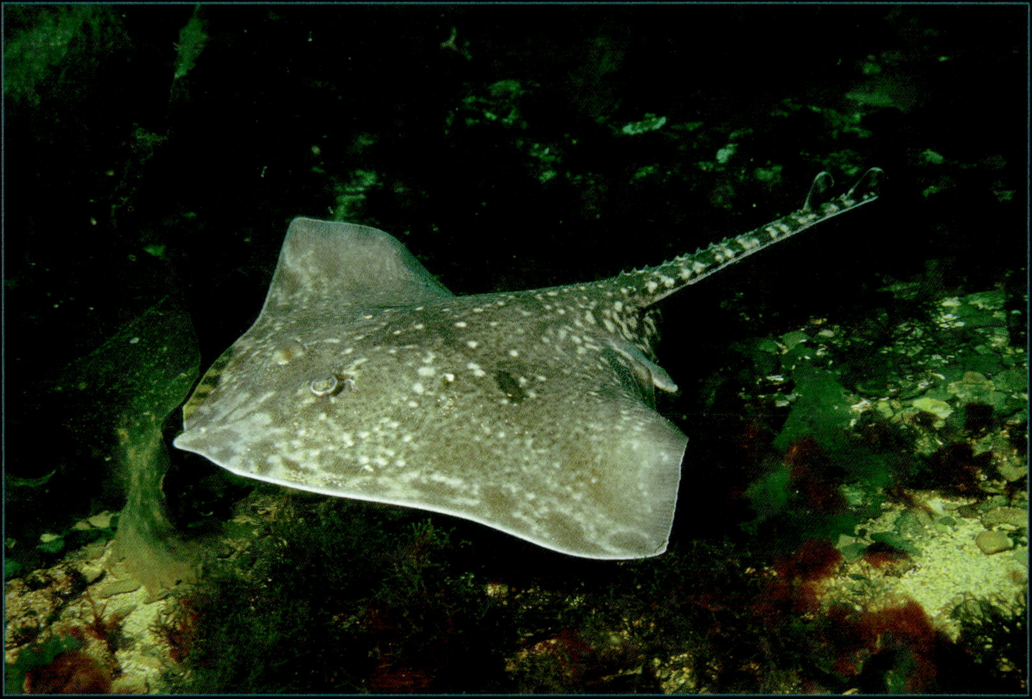

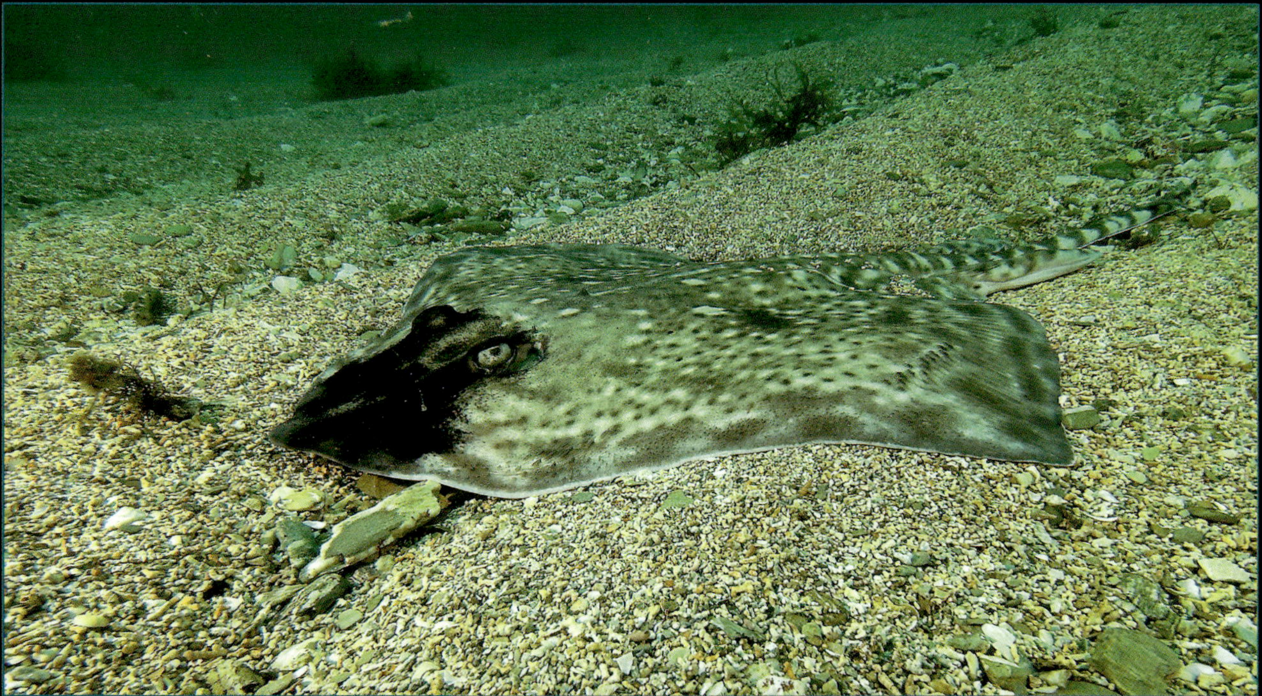

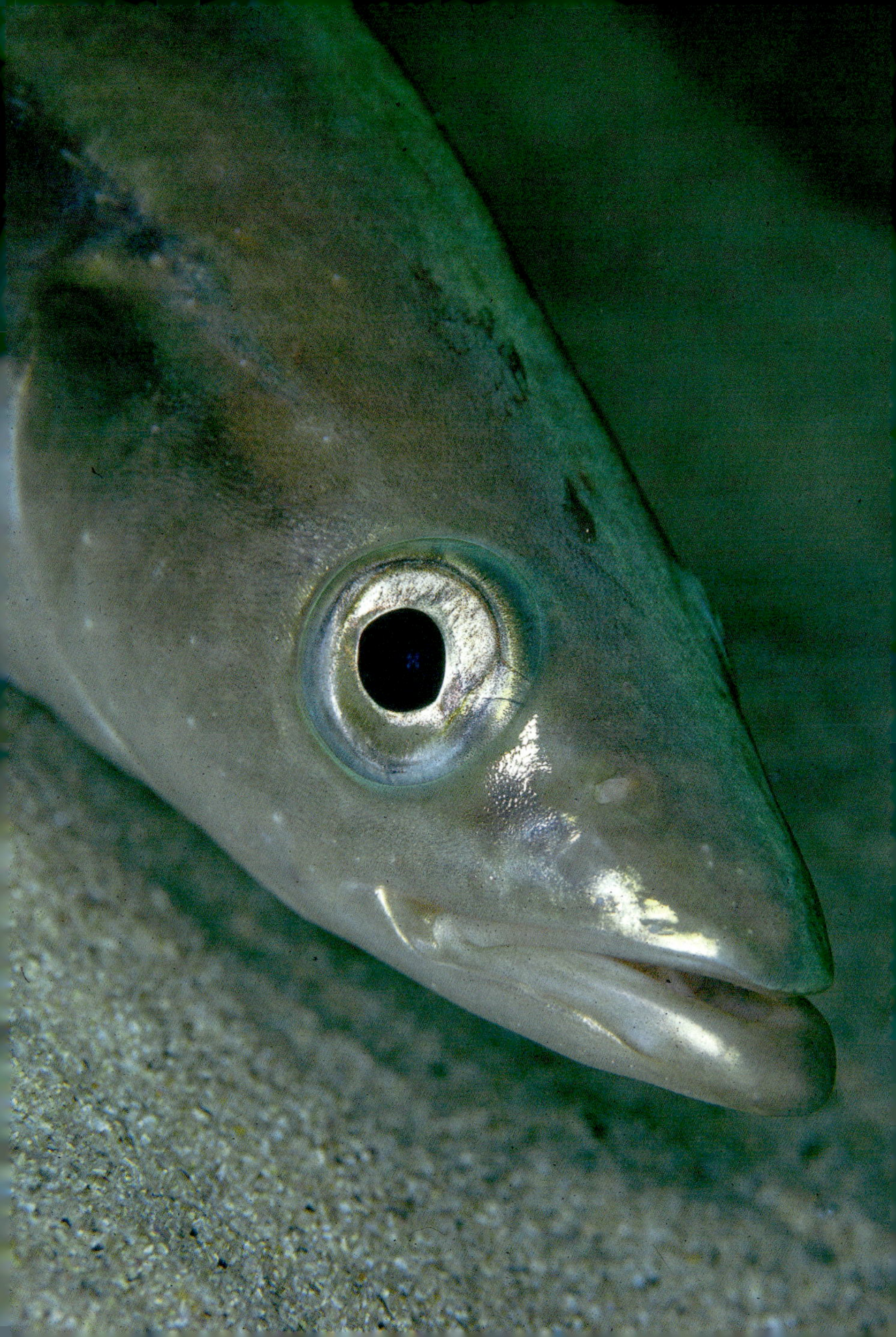

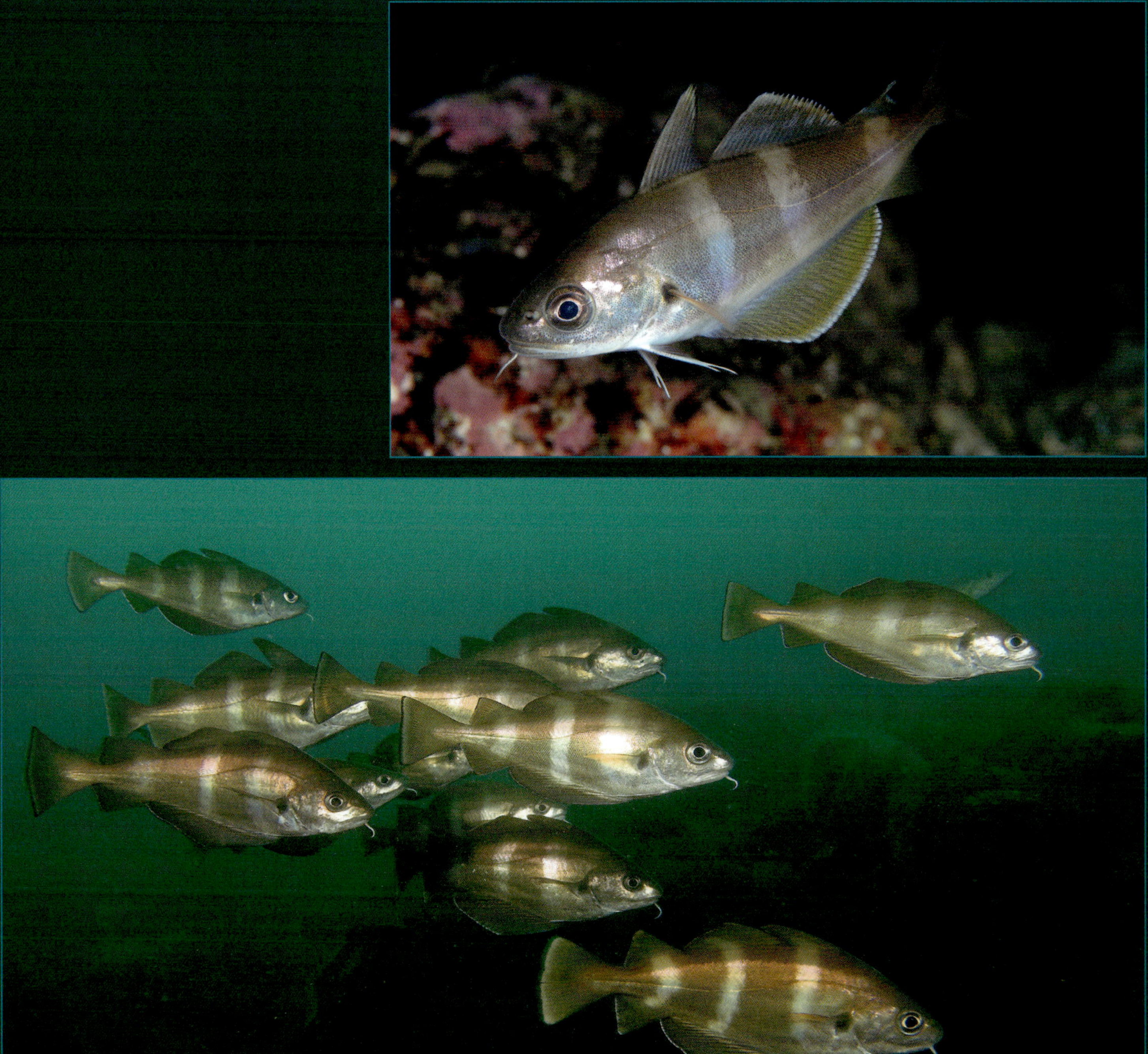

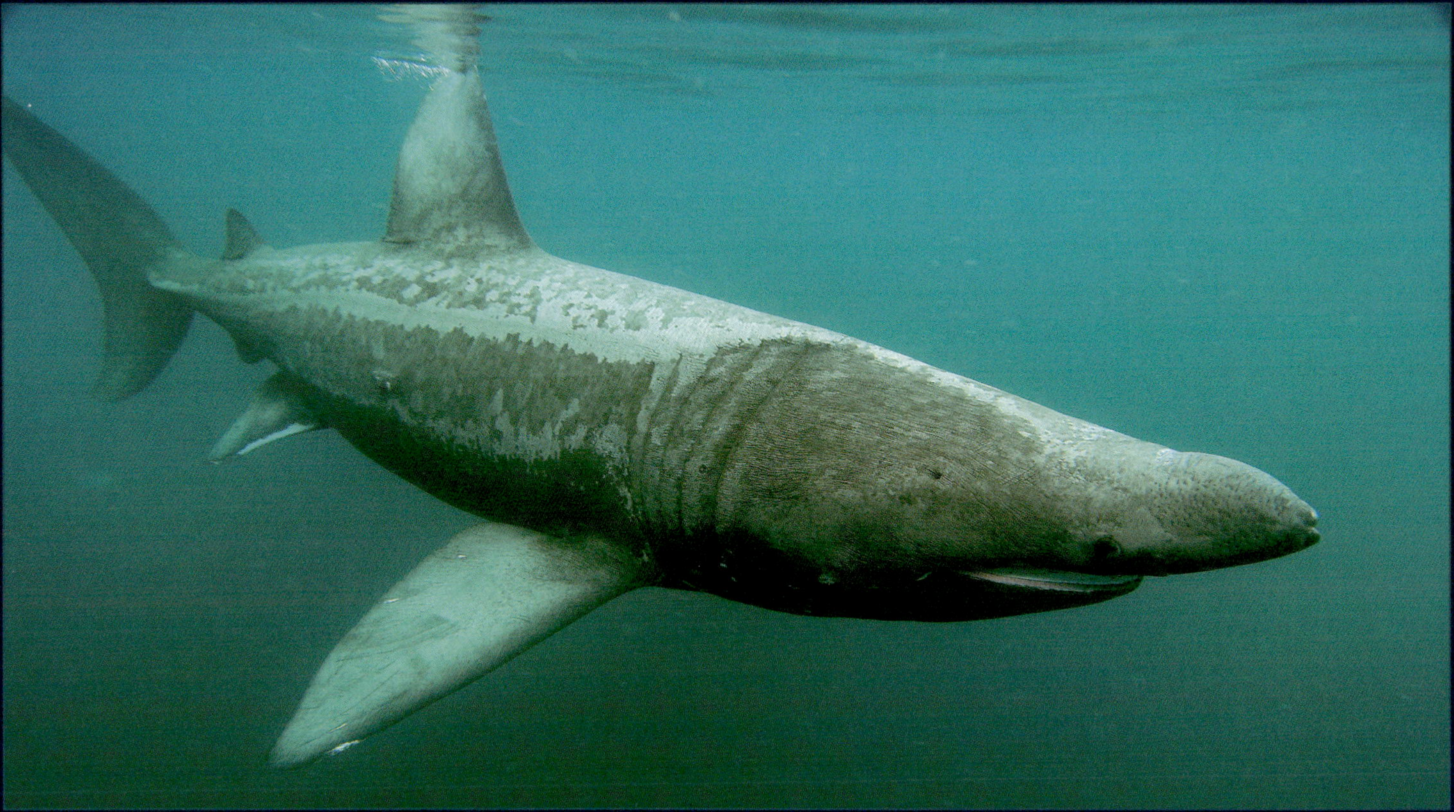

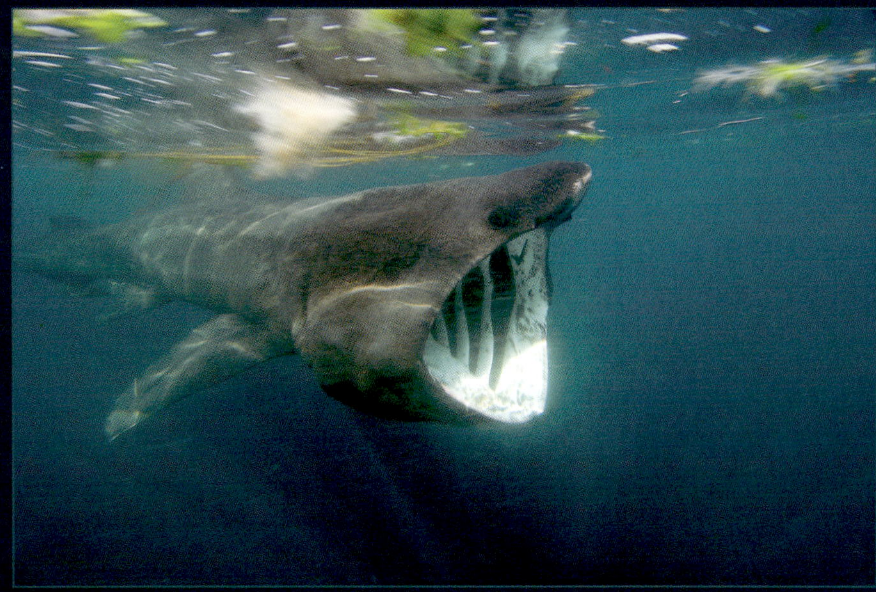

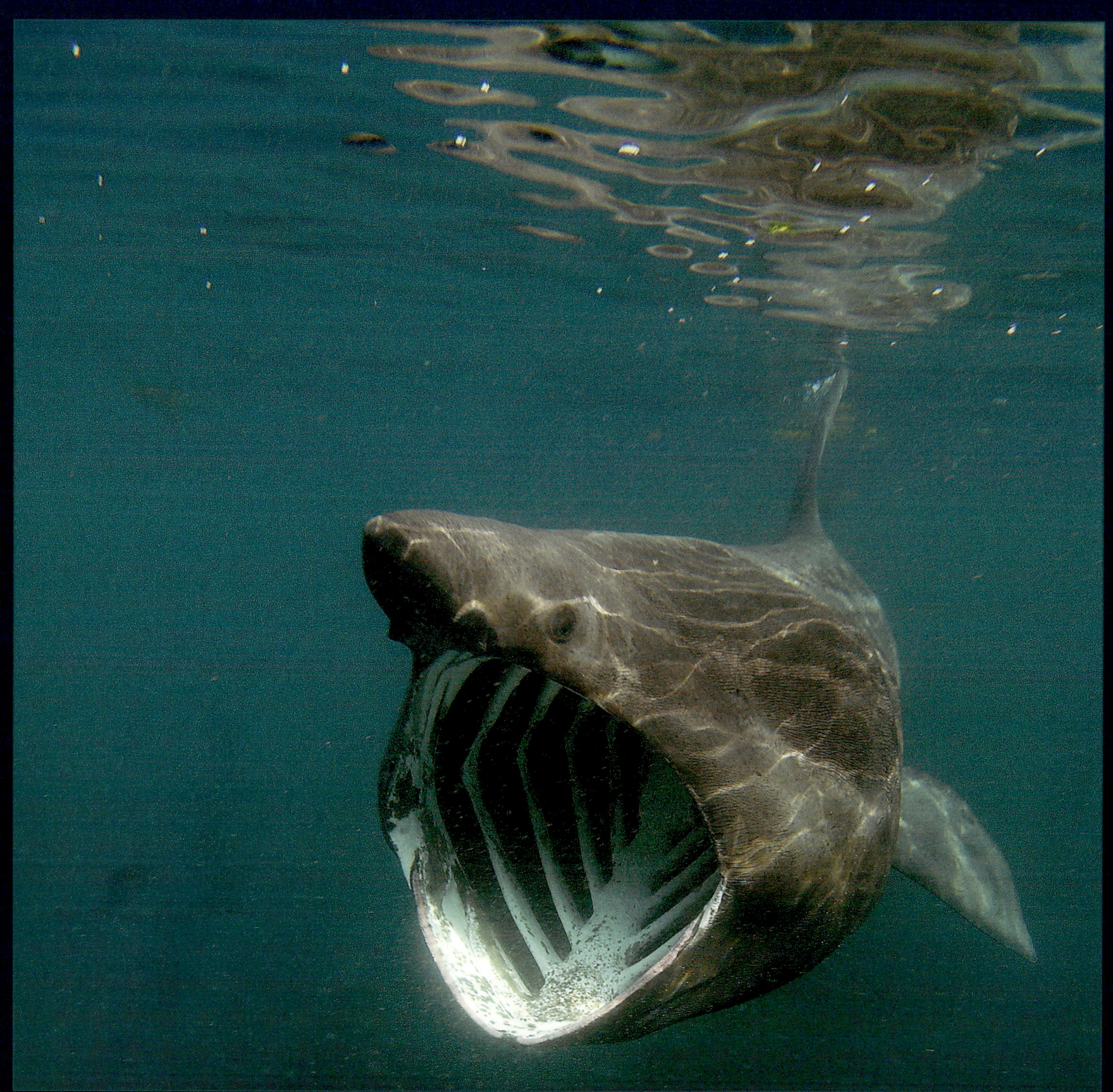

Basking shark

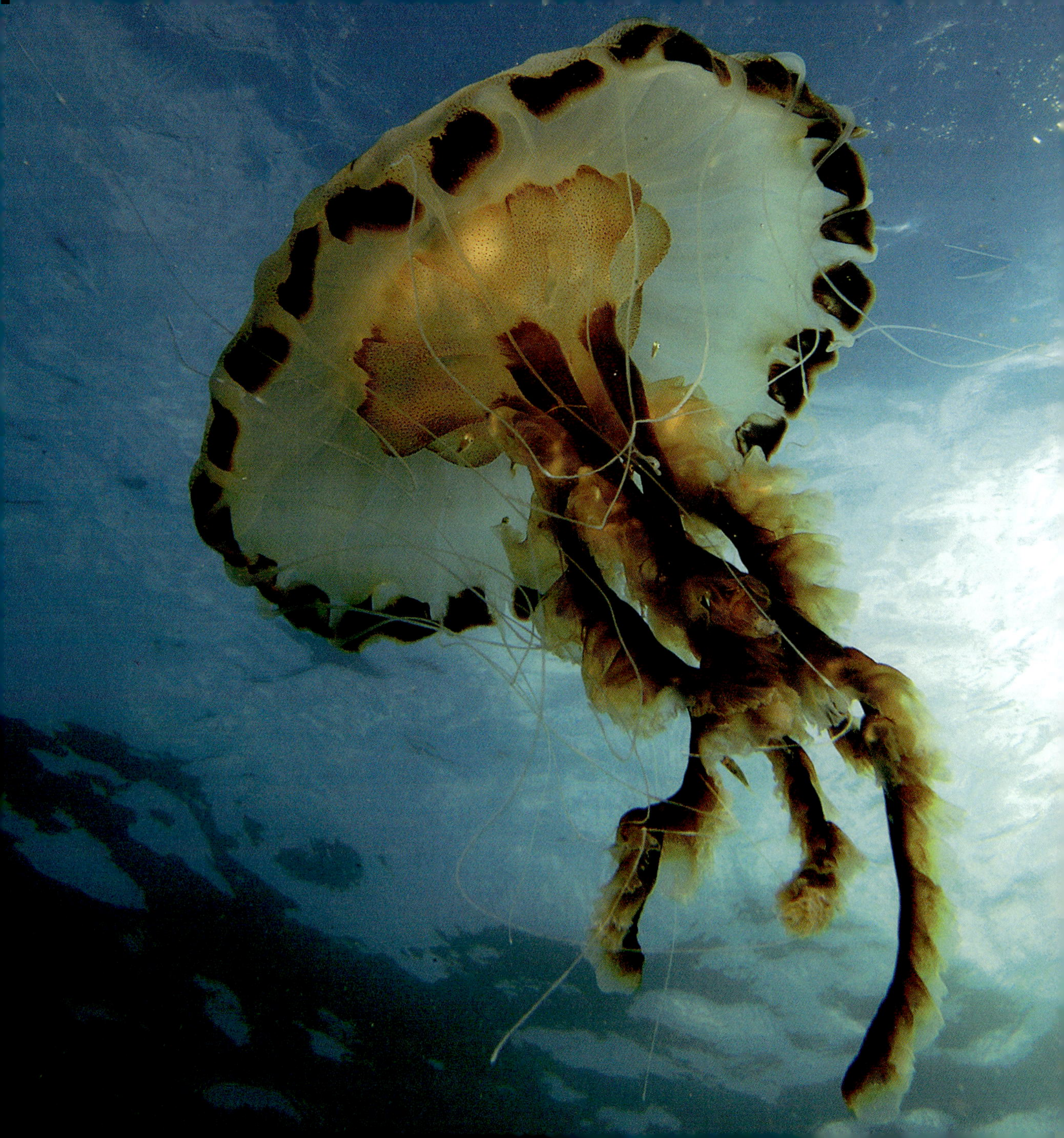

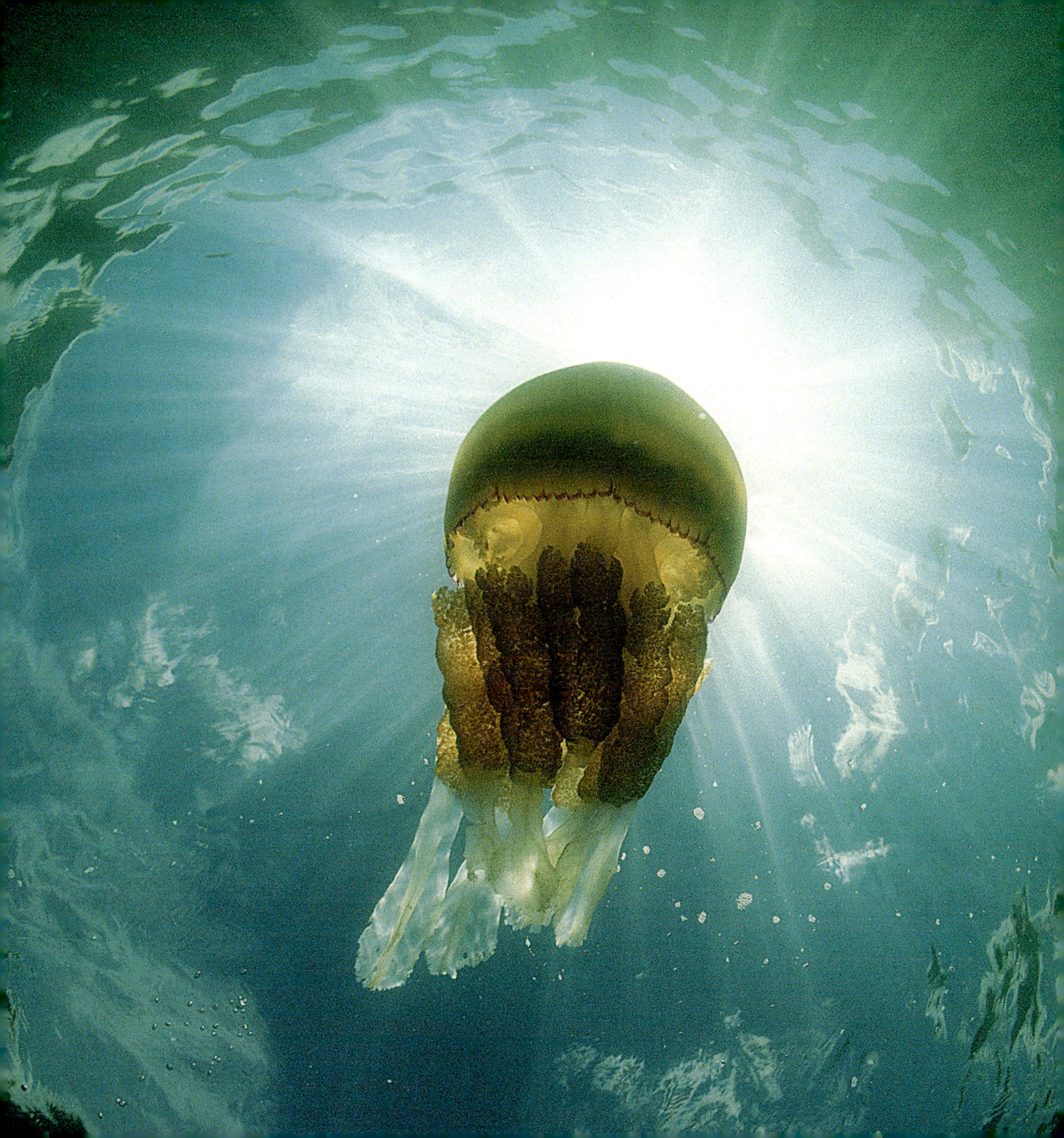

Notes and technical details

PAGE 1: The eye of this Corkwing wrasse (*Crenilabrus melops*) illustrates the intricate pattern of blue and red which this fish develops when reaching adulthood. Porthkerris Cove, Lizard. Nikon F90X, Subal housing, 105 mm macro, Inon Quad flash gun, Fujichrome Velvia 50 ASA, f16 1/60.

PAGE 3: Taking the plunge under the water with SCUBA equipment (self-contained breathing apparatus) reveals an amazing new world and allows you to explore in three dimensions. Here a diver explores a gully with walls carpeted in soft corals known as dead men's fingers (*Alcyonium digitatum*). You will need the correct training and equipment to dive safely. Logan Rock, Purthcurno Bay. Nikon F90X, Subal housing, 16 mm fisheye, YS120 and YS30 flash guns, Fujichrome Velvia 50 ASA, f5.6 1/30.

PAGE 5: Snorkelling in Cornwall is possible from almost any beach. However, the most productive are the small coves and bays with a rocky foreshore and fringing reef, which will allow you to get close to marine life in shallow water. Pendennis Point, Falmouth. Nikon D200, Subal housing, 10.5 mm fisheye, ISO 100 f8 1/60.

PAGE 6: An inquisitive ballan wrasse (*Labrus bergylta*) peers out from multi-coloured seaweeds at Pendennis Point, Falmouth. Nikon D300, Subal housing, 12–24 mm zoom, Subtronic, Mini flash guns, ISO 200 f11 1/60.

PAGES 10–11: During calm weather in early autumn leaves and seaweeds are carried down the Helford River towards Falmouth Bay. Calm, sunny conditions allow an image to be taken through the water surface, including the trees and river bank in the background. Nikon D200, Subal housing, 18–35 mm zoom, ISO 100 f11 1/60.

PAGES 12–13: The fringing reefs are often cut by deep gullies topped by a kelp forest. These swim-throughs are exciting to explore, and are home to a wide variety of fish, crustaceans and invertebrates. Minack Reef, Porthcurno Bay. Nikon D200, Subal housing, 12–24 mm zoom, Subtronic Mini flash guns, ISO 100 f8 1/60.

PAGE 14: These Daisy anemones (*Sagartia elegans*) are a dramatic contrast to the bright red encrusting algae. This species is common on all shallow elevations of inshore and offshore reefs. Prussia Cove, Mount's Bay. Nikon D100, Light and Motion housing, 105 mm macro, Inon Quad flash gun, ISO 200 f16 1/125.

PAGE 14: Dahlia anemones (*Urticina felina*) come in a range of colours which seem to get more vivid when the species is exposed to strong currents that carry the nutrients they feed on. Runnel Stone, Land's End. Nikon F90X, Subal housing, 60 mm macro, YS50 and YS30 flash guns, Fujichrome Velvia 50 ASA, f16 1/60.

PAGE 15: Strawberry anemones (*Actinia fragacea*) have amazingly vivid colours and derive their common name from the spots on the mantle which is normally hidden when the anemone is fully extended to feed. They are found mostly in rock pools and rocky foreshores. Porthkerris Cove, Lizard. Nikon D100, Light and Motion housing, 105 mm macro, Inon Quad flash gun, ISO 200 f16 1/125.

PAGE 16: A tiny hermit crab scales a blade of eel grass. Beds of eel grass are found in Mount's Bay, the Helford River and Carrick Roads close to St Mawes. This is a Mediterranean species which is able to thrive here due to the warming waters of the Gulf Stream. These beds provide ideal breeding grounds and a nursery environment for many species. Durgan, Helford River. Nikon D100, Light and Motion housing, 105 mm macro, Inon Quad flash gun, ISO 200 f16 1/125.

PAGE 16: Common prawns (*Palaemon serratus*) like the darker recesses of the reef and are often found in small groups crammed into a crack or fissure in the reef wall. Pendennis Point, Falmouth. Nikon D100, Light and Motion housing, 105 mm macro, Inon Quad flash gun, ISO 200 f16 1/125.

PAGE 17: Tropical anemones are well known for their symbiotic relationships with crustaceans and some fish species. A Cornish example is the snakelocks anemone (*Anemonia viridis*) and Leach's spider crab (*Inachus phalangium*) – the crab gains the protection of the anemone and presumably shares meals as well. Both are found in shallow waters on the reef edge, and often in deeper rock pools. Pendennis Point, Falmouth. Nikon D100, Light and Motion housing, 105 mm macro, Inon Quad flash gun, ISO 200 f16 1/125.

PAGE 17: In some coastal areas the common lobster can be very difficult to find, due to heavy fishing to meet demand from the restaurant trade and overseas markets. The National Lobster Hatchery in Padstow grows juveniles to a size at which they can be released back into the wild to repopulate the reefs. Pendennis Point, Falmouth. Nikon D200, Subal housing, 12–24 mm zoom, Subtronic Mini flash guns, ISO 100 f11 1/60.

PAGE 18 and front cover: Long- and short-spined scorpion fish are common in shallow waters and rock pools, but are often difficult to spot due to their excellent camouflage. They are able to change colour to suit their background and to hide from potential prey. This long-spined (*Taurulus bubalis*) example has purple livery to match the calcified seaweed it is resting on. Prussia Cove, Mount's Bay. Nikon F2, Hugyfot housing, 55 mm macro, YS50 flash gun, Kodachrome 64 ASA, f11 1/60.

PAGE 18: This short-spined scorpion fish (*Myoxocephalus scorpius*) is decorated with pink and red patches to match encrusting algaes and the red seaweeds of shallow waters. Porthkerris Cove, Lizard. Nikon F90X, Subal housing, 60 mm macro, YS50 and YS30 flash guns, Fujichrome Velvia 50 ASA, f16 1/60.

PAGE 19: This long-spined scorpion fish (*Taurulus bubalis*) has a colour and pattern more in tune with the brown and green seaweeds found in rock pools. Pendennis Point, Falmouth. Nikon D100, Light and Motion housing, 105 mm macro, Inon Quad flash gun, ISO 200 f16 1/125.

PAGE 20: One of the most colourful, comical-looking and inquisitive fish on the reef is the tompot blenny (*Parablennius gattorugine*). These fish are very territorial and live for many years in the same hole on the reef. This is one I have been visiting just off Pendennis Point, Falmouth, for more than five years. Nikon D200, Subal housing, 105 mm macro, Inon Quad flash gun, ISO 100 f16 1/125.

PAGE 21: The shanny (*Lipophrys pholis*) is often seen in a few centimetres of water or in rock pools between the tides. It is an inquisitive fish and will come very close once you have its confidence. Pendennis Point, Falmouth. Nikon F90X, Subal housing, 105 mm macro, Inon Quad flash gun, Fujichrome Velvia 50 ASA, f11 1/60.

PAGE 21: Three species of pipefish are commonly seen in Cornish waters. This is the largest, the greater pipefish (*Syngnathus acus*). They have very good camouflage and are most often found moving through seaweeds on the seabed where they feed on small shrimp and fish. Pendennis Point, Falmouth. Nikon D200, Subal housing, 105 mm macro, Inon Quad flash gun, ISO 100 f11 1/80.

PAGE 22: The Blood Henry starfish (*Henricia oculata*) is very common on shallow reefs and easily spotted due to its vivid pink to purple colour. Porthkerris Cove, Lizard. Nikon F90X, Subal housing, 60 mm macro, YS50 and YS30 flash guns, Fujichrome Velvia 50 ASA, f16 1/60.

PAGE 22 (middle): A detailed close-up image of the Blood Henry starfish (*Henricia oculata*) shows the intricate texture of this species. Pendennis Point, Falmouth. Nikon D200, Subal housing, 105 mm macro, Inon Quad flash gun, ISO 100 f11 1/80.

PAGE 22: One of the most exotic-looking starfish is the red cushion star (*Porania pulvillus*). It is found on deeper reefs where it feeds on soft corals (dead men's fingers –*Alcyonium digitatum*). Low Lee Reef, Mount's Bay. Nikon F90X, Subal housing, 60 mm macro, YS50 and YS30 flash guns, Fujichrome Velvia 50 ASA, f11 1/60.

PAGE 23: The spiny starfish (*Marthasterias glacialis*) is covered with knobs and spines to protect itself against predators. It is seen in a variety of colours, with different colours highlighting the spines. Pendennis Point, Falmouth. Nikon D200, Subal housing, 105 mm macro, Inon Quad flash gun, ISO 100 f11 1/80.

PAGE 24: One of the strangest-looking fish in Cornish waters is found only in early spring. The lumpsucker (*Cyclopterus lumpus*) comes into shallow water to breed, and the male is left for up to four weeks to guard and tend the egg mass, which is often laid in a crack on the reef, or frequently on wrecks. Low Lee Reef, Mount's Bay. Nikon F801, Subal housing, 16 mm fisheye, Subatec S100 flash gun, Fujichrome Velvia 50 ASA, f11 1/60.

PAGE 25: A close-up of the male lumpsucker (*Cyclopterus lumpus*) reveals its strange features, and the bright orange colour that it develops during the breeding season. For the rest of the year it is a dull green/brown colour. Low Lee Reef, Mount's Bay. Nikon F801, Subal housing, 60 mm macro, YS50 and YS30 flash guns, Fujichrome Velvia 50 ASA, f16 1/60.

PAGE 26: Conger eels (*Conger conger*) are found on shallow and deep reefs, and particularly on wrecks where there are plenty of holes for them to hide. Although they have a fearsome reputation with fishermen, they are mostly docile and inquisitive when found underwater. Minack Reef, Porthcurno Bay. Nikon D200, Subal housing, 12–24 mm zoom, Subtronic Mini flash guns, ISO 100 f11 1/60.

PAGE 27: The warmer waters of the Gulf Stream occasionally bring visitors from much further south in the Atlantic. The grey Atlantic trigger fish (*Balistes carolinensis*) is one of these. It is more associated with semi-tropical temperatures, but is often seen after a long hot summer in September and October, particularly in the Land's End area. Minack Reef, Porthcurno Bay. Nikon F90X, Subal housing, 18–35mm zoom, YS120 and YS30 flash guns, Fujichrome Velvia 50 ASA, f16 1/60.

PAGE 28: Cuttlefish (*Sepia officinalis*) are members of the cephalopod family. They are common around shallow reefs, but difficult to see due to their mastery of camouflage. They are able to change pattern, colour and texture in a moment, but if you are patient they will come very close and show great interest in what you are up to. Porthkerris Cove, Lizard. Nikon F801, Subal housing, 60 mm macro, YS50 and YS30 flash guns, Fujichrome Velvia 50 ASA, f16 1/60.

PAGE 29: Cuttlefish (*Sepia officinalis*) often use colour and pattern to communicate with each other, particularly during their mating season in springtime. This striped pattern is very common in courting males. Pendennis Point, Falmouth. Nikon D100, Light and Motion housing, 12–24 mm zoom, Subtronic Mini flash guns, ISO 200 f11 1/60.

PAGE 29: In late summer the juvenile cuttlefish (*Sepia officinalis*) begin to appear, and can often be found in large groups on certain reefs. Like all youngsters they are very inquisitive, and will pose for the camera. Porthkerris Cove, Lizard. Nikon D100, Light and Motion housing, 105 mm macro, Inon Quad flash gun, ISO 200 f11 1/60.

PAGE 30: One of the most spectacular fish in our waters is the John Dory (*Zeus faber*), or St Peter fish. This is supposedly the fish that St Peter plucked from the water, leaving a dark circle on each flank where his fingers gripped the fish. Pendennis Point, Falmouth. Nikon F90X, Subal housing, 105 mm macro, Inon Quad flash gun, Fujichrome Velvia 50 ASA, f11 1/125.

PAGE 31: The John Dory (*Zeus faber*) has excellent camouflage and a thin body shape for hiding and hunting among seaweeds. It is also shy, so is very difficult to find and photograph. Pendennis Point, Falmouth. Nikon D100, Light and Motion housing, 18–35 mm zoom, Subtronic Mini flash guns, ISO 200 f11 1/60.

PAGE 32: Juvenile corkwing wrasse (*Crenilabrus melops*) are often found among the eel grass in the Helford estuary with many other species of juvenile fish. They move further out on to the reefs once they have grown large enough to defend themselves. Durgan, Helford River. Nikon F90X, Subal housing, 105 mm macro, Inon Quad flash gun, Fujichrome Velvia 50 ASA, f11 1/125.

PAGE 32: Black gobies (*Gobius niger*) are often seen at the bottom of the reef where it joins the sand or gravel seabed. They are quite abundant, although their mottled pattern blends well with the seabed. Pendennis Point, Falmouth. Nikon D100, Light and Motion housing, 105 mm macro, Inon Quad flash gun, ISO 200 f11 1/80.

PAGE 33: Male Ballan wrasse (*Labrus bergylta*) are perhaps the largest and most colourful of the fish found on our inshore reefs. They are quite territorial and will keep returning to the same spot on a reef if you are patient enough to wait. They often hide among kelp and weed to peek out at you. Pendennis Point, Falmouth. Nikon F90X, Subal housing, 105 mm macro, Inon Quad flash gun, Fujichrome Velvia 50 ASA, f8 1/60.

PAGE 33: Ballan wrasse (*Labrus bergylta*) yawning – these fish can often be seen scooping up mouthfuls of sand or gravel to eat small crustaceans. They sift the gravel in their mouths and then spit it out, but every now and then need a good yawn to expel those final little bits. Porthkerris Cove, Lizard. Nikon F90X, Subal housing, 105 mm macro, Inon Quad flash gun, Fujichrome Velvia 50 ASA, f8 1/60.

PAGE 34: On the offshore reefs the most colourful species of wrasse is the male cuckoo wrasse (*Labrus bimaculatus*), with its splendid blue and orange livery. All cuckoo wrasse, like their close relatives ballan wrasse, start life as females. The dominant and more colourful male will command an area of reef until he is predated or dies, when the next most dominant female will begin the sex change to male. Low Lee Reef, Mount's Bay. Nikon D200, Subal housing, 12–24 mm zoom, Subtronic Mini flash guns, ISO 100 f11 1/60.

PAGE 35: The male cuckoo wrasse (*Labrus bimaculatus*) is very bold when a diver enters its territory, and will often swim right up to your mask or the port of the camera housing, most likely challenging its own reflection. Low Lee Reef, Mount's Bay. Nikon F90X, Subal housing, 60 mm macro, YS50 and YS30 flash guns, Fujichrome Velvia 50 ASA, f11 1/125.

PAGE 35: Monkfish or angler fish (*Lophius piscatorius*) are among the most bizarre-looking bottom-dwellers, and can grow to more than a metre (3 ft) in length. They are ambush predators, and lie motionless on the seabed until a meal swims by, when they open their enormous mouths and suck in their hapless prey. Porthkerris Cove, Lizard. Nikon F90X, Subal housing, 60 mm macro, YS50 and YS30 flash guns, Fujichrome Velvia 50 ASA, f11 1/125.

PAGE 36: Kelp (*Laminaria* sp.) forests dominate the reef tops on both inshore and offshore reefs. This is an extremely tough plant that hangs on to the reef top with a root system called 'holdfasts' which can withstand rough seas. Logan's Gully, Porthcurno Bay. Nikon D100, Light and Motion housing, 10.5 mm fisheye, Subtronic Mini flash guns, ISO 200 f11 1/60.

PAGE 37: The constant movement of seawater by tides and swells moves the seaweeds (*Laminaria* sp.) and sometimes results in attractive patterns or swirls like this one. Pendennis Point, Falmouth. Nikon D100, Light and Motion housing, 105 mm macro, Inon Quad flash gun, ISO 200 f11 1/80.

PAGE 38: This juvenile common starfish (*Asterias rubens*) is climbing an eel grass stalk, perhaps grazing on algae. Exploring the eel grass beds in the Helford River reveals all sorts of juvenile species. Durgan, Helford River. Nikon D100, Light and Motion housing, 105 mm macro, Inon Quad flash gun, ISO 200 f11 1/80.

PAGE 39: Small snakelocks anemones (*Anemonia viridis*) are often found on the eel grass stalks in the Helford River from March to November. When the winter storms arrive, both are swept away. Durgan, Helford River. Nikon D100, Light and Motion housing, 105 mm macro, Inon Quad flash gun, ISO 200 f11 1/80.

PAGE 40: Common spiny sea urchins (*Echinus esculentus*) are found frequently in depths of 10–25 m (33–82 ft). They appear in a variety of colours, and for many years were collected for the tourist curio trade for lamps or decoration. Moving in close reveals the intricate construction of these creatures. Pendennis Point, Falmouth. Nikon D200, Subal housing, 105 mm macro, Inon Quad flash gun, ISO 100 f16 1/125.

PAGE 40: Worms on land conjure up a quite unpleasant image. Underwater sessile, reef-dwelling worms have beautiful, plume-like gills that they extend from their burrows or tube homes. This fan worm (*Bispira volutacornis*) has delicate plumes which are sensitive to shadow and movement and will retract quickly, so it can be difficult to photograph. Pendennis Point, Falmouth. Nikon D100, Light and Motion housing, 105 mm macro, Inon Quad flash gun, ISO 200 f11 1/80.

PAGE 41: There are numerous species of sea squirts (*Ascidia mentula*) on the reef. These simple creatures filter seawater for nutrients, while growing in colonies on the kelp stypes or on the reef. Pendennis Point, Falmouth. Nikon D100, Light and Motion housing, 105 mm macro, Inon Quad flash gun, ISO 200 f11 1/80.

PAGE 42: One of the prettiest anemones to be found is also the smallest. Jewel anemones (*Corynactis viridis*) thrive on exposed rock faces where there are strong currents, and so are found mostly on offshore reefs like the Manacles and Runnel Stone. Raglans Reef, Manacles, Falmouth Bay. Nikon D100, Light and Motion housing, 105 mm macro, Inon Quad flash gun, ISO 200 f16 1/80.

PAGE 43: A diver examines a colony of jewel anemones (*Corynactis viridis*). These anemones always grow together in colonies, sometimes covering large areas of reef. Each group will be dominated by a particular colour, ranging from pinks, yellows and blues to deep purples. Raglans Reef, Manacles, Falmouth Bay. Nikon F90X, Subal housing, 16 mm fisheye, YS120 and YS30 flash guns, Fujichrome Velvia 50ASA, f8 1/30.

PAGE 43: Bright pink jewel anemones (*Corynactis viridis*) make a very attractive photographic subject. Perhaps 12 mm (0.5 in) in diameter, they need a close-up or macro lens to capture the detail. Raglans Reef, Manacles, Falmouth Bay. Nikon D100, Light and Motion housing, 105 mm macro, Inon Quad flash gun, ISO 200 f16 1/80.

PAGE 44: A colony of the brightly coloured soft coral 'red fingers' (*Alcyonium glomeratum*) thrives on reef areas exposed to the tides and currents that carry the planktonic nutrients they feed on. Low Lee Reef, Mount's Bay. Nikon D100, Light and Motion housing, 10.5 mm fisheye, Subtronic Mini flash guns, ISO 200 f8 1/30.

PAGE 44: The more common species of soft coral 'dead men's fingers' (*Alcyonium digitatum*) range in colour from brilliant white to a pale yellow, and are a common sight on offshore reefs exposed to tidal flow. Low Lee Reef, Mount's Bay. Nikon D100, Light and Motion housing, 10.5 mm fisheye, Subtronic Mini flash guns, ISO 200 f8 1/30.

PAGE 45: The delicate polyps of 'red fingers' soft coral (*Alcyonium glomeratum*) are revealed in close-up. The individual polyps form part of a much larger colonial animal, and are closely related to the tropical species of soft coral. Logan Rock, Porthcurno Bay. Nikon D200, Subal housing, 105 mm macro, Inon Quad flash gun, ISO 100 f16 1/125.

PAGE 46: Hermit crabs (*Pagurus bernhardus*) lack the tough outer shell that most other crabs have, and consequently have to find a suitable vacant shell to carry with them for protection. As they grow they need to trade up to a larger shell. Helford River. Nikon D200, Subal housing, 105 mm macro, Inon Quad flash gun, ISO 100 f11 1/80.

PAGE 46: The common edible crab (*Cancer pagurus*) is seen on almost every dive, although large examples are now extremely rare due to the heavy fishing for this species. Pendennis Point, Falmouth. Nikon D200, Subal housing, 105 mm macro, Inon Quad flash gun, ISO 100 f11 1/80.

PAGE 47: Spider crabs (*Maja squinado*) are seen on inshore and offshore reefs, and often on the sand. They sometimes decorate their shells with weed and sponges as camouflage. They are fished commercially, with most of the catch exported to Europe. Logan Rock, Porthcurno Bay. Nikon D100, Light and Motion housing, 10.5 mm fisheye, Subtronic Mini flash guns, ISO 200 f8 1/30.

PAGE 48: Some of the largest anemones to be seen are the plumose variety (*Metridium senile*), which are coloured in pastel shades ranging from orange and yellow to green and white. Logan's Gully, Porthcurno Bay. Nikon D100, Light and Motion housing, 10.5 mm fisheye, Subtronic Mini flash guns, ISO 200 f16 1/30.

PAGE 49: Plumose anemones (*Metridium senile*) grow in large colonies on exposed offshore reefs. The display of colour is more like what you would expect to see on a tropical reef than in cool Cornish waters. Logan's Gully, Porthcurno Bay. Nikon D100, Light and Motion housing, 10.5 mm fisheye, Subtronic Mini flash guns, ISO 200 f16 1/30.

PAGE 49: Plumose anemones (*Metridium senile*) can reach a height of 30 cm (1 ft) when extended to feed in the current. When the tidal flow stops and begins to turn, they often deflate completely and close up to small blobs on the reef. Logan's Gully, Porthcurno Bay. Nikon D100, Light and Motion housing, 10.5 mm fisheye,

Subtronic Mini flash guns, ISO 200 f16 1/30.

PAGE 50: Corkwing wrasse (*Crenilabrus melops*) are seen throughout the year on inshore reefs. In spring the male can be observed collecting pieces of seaweed and debris to build a nest on the reef in preparation for breeding. Once the eggs have been laid and fertilized the male will guard them until they hatch. Porthkerris Cove, Lizard. Nikon D100, Light and Motion housing, 105 mm macro, Inon Quad flash gun, ISO 200 f16 1/80.

PAGE 51: The Corkwing wrasse (*Crenilabrus melops*) does not appear to undergo a sex change, unlike other species of wrasse. However, a young male that has yet to develop a territory or breed has subdued colouration, more like the female, until it matures. Pendennis Point, Falmouth. Nikon D100, Light and Motion housing, 105 mm macro, Inon Quad flash gun, ISO 200 f16 1/80.

PAGE 52: Numerous species of gobies are to be found on inshore reefs, one of the most striking being the leopard-spotted goby (*Thorogobius ephippiatus*), which generally sits at the front of its burrow on the reef edge. Pendennis Point, Falmouth. Nikon D100, Light and Motion housing, 105 mm macro, Inon Quad flash gun, ISO 200 f16 1/80.

PAGE 53: Two-spot gobies (*Gobiusculus flavescens*) are normally seen in small schools swimming above the kelp on inshore reefs. During the winter they become much more sedentary, and are often found resting on seaweeds and hydroids. Pendennis Point, Falmouth. Nikon D100, Light and Motion housing, 105 mm macro, Inon Quad flash gun, ISO 200 f16 1/80.

PAGE 54: Sea slugs or nudibranchs (this species *Diaphorodoris luteocincta*) are much more colourful than their terrestrial cousins, and are in fact molluscs that have discarded their shells as they evolved. Low Lee Reef, Mount's Bay. Nikon D100, Light and Motion housing, 105 mm macro, Inon Quad flash gun, ISO 200 f16 1/30.

PAGE 55: Sea slugs or nudibranchs (this species *Polycera quadrilineata*) lay their eggs in early spring, quite often on the fronds of kelp seaweed. Minack Reef, Porthcurno Bay. Nikon D100, Light and Motion housing, 105 mm macro, Inon Quad flash gun, ISO 200 f16 1/30.

PAGE 56: Some sea slugs (this species *Coryphella browni*) lay their eggs in intricate patterns on kelp fronds. The eggs are generally white, but occasionally you will find coloured clusters, depending on what the species has been feeding on. Minack Reef, Porthcurno Bay. Nikon D100, Light and Motion housing, 105 mm macro, Inon Quad flash gun, ISO 200 f16 1/60.

PAGE 57: Sea slugs (this species *Limacia clavigera*) often feed on algae that grows on various seaweeds. Some species also feed on stinging hydroids, and retain the stinging cells in their cerata (body appendages) to discourage predators. Pendennis Point, Falmouth. Nikon D100, Light and Motion housing, 105 mm macro, Inon Quad flash gun, ISO 200 f16 1/125.

PAGE 58: One of the most abundant sea anemones found on shallow-water reefs is the snakelocks (*Anemonia viridis*), which makes a very attractive photographic subject. Pendennis Point, Falmouth. Nikon D100, Light and Motion housing, 18–35 mm zoom, Subtronic Mini flash guns, ISO 200 f8 1/30.

PAGE 59: The snakelocks anemone (*Anemonia viridis*) often has a hidden partner – the Leach's spider crab (*Inachus phalangium*), which lives in symbiosis with the anemone and is unaffected by its sting. Pendennis Point, Falmouth. Nikon D100, Light and Motion housing, 105 mm macro, Inon Quad flash gun, ISO 200 f16 1/125.

PAGE 59: Scallops (*Pecten maximus*) are most often found on silty or sandy seabeds, and are a valuable commercial catch. Unfortunately, the dredging method used to catch them does great damage to surrounding marine habitats. Pendennis Point, Falmouth. Nikon D200, Subal housing, 18–35 mm zoom, Subtronic Mini flash guns, ISO 100 f8 1/30.

PAGE 60: The lesser-spotted dogfish (*Scyliorhinus canicula*) is a small member of the shark family, and feeds mostly on small crustaceans and fish. Pendennis Point, Falmouth. Nikon D200, Subal housing, 18–35 mm zoom, Subtronic Mini flash guns, ISO 100 f11 1/80.

PAGE 61: The lesser-spotted dogfish (*Scyliorhinus canicula*) are nocturnal hunters, and during the day are often found resting or sleeping on the seabed, making them very easy to approach and photograph. Pendennis Point, Falmouth. Nikon D200, Subal housing, 12–24 mm zoom, Subtronic Mini flash guns, ISO 100 f11 1/15.

PAGE 62: Spider crabs (*Maja squinado*) are often observed in late spring or early summer marching across the seabed towards shallow water where they congregate in significant numbers to breed. Pendennis Point, Falmouth. Nikon D100, Light and Motion housing, 12–24 mm zoom, Subtronic Mini flash guns, ISO 200 f11 1/30.

PAGE 62: Shore crabs (*Carcinus maenas*) are found in rock pools, on inshore reefs and in estuaries. In soft seabeds they will often bury themselves completely, but if disturbed become very pugnacious and have no fear of a diver. Helford River. Nikon D100, Light and Motion housing, 105 mm macro, Inon Quad flash gun, ISO 200 f16 1/125.

PAGE 63: This alien-looking face belongs to the squat lobster (*Galathea strigosa*), which can be found in almost any crack or fissure on an inshore reef. The flash illuminates its vivid red and blue colouration. Pendennis Point, Falmouth. Nikon D100, Light and Motion housing, 105 mm macro, Inon Quad flash gun, ISO 200 f16 1/125.

PAGE 63: Velvet swimming crabs (*Necora puber*) are not often observed swimming. They are most active at night, when their ability to swim allows them to capture fast-moving prey such as prawns and small fish. Pendennis Point, Falmouth. Nikon D200, Subal housing, 105 mm macro, Inon Quad flash gun, ISO 100 f16 1/60.

PAGE 64: Topknot flat fish (*Zeugopterus punctatus*) are unusual in that they prefer to reside on the reef rather than sandy seabeds that many other species prefer. St Clement's Island, Mousehole. Nikon F801, Subal housing, 60 mm macro, YS50 and YS30 flash guns, Fujichrome Velvia 50 ASA, f11 1/60.

PAGE 64: Topknot flat fish (*Zeugopterus punctatus*) have terrific camouflage, and blend perfectly with the reef surface. Occasionally they can be captured when free-swimming, which highlights their weird features. Pendennis Point, Falmouth. Nikon F801, Subal housing, 60 mm macro, YS50 and YS30 flash guns, Fujichrome Velvia 50 ASA, f11 1/60.

PAGE 65: Topknot flat fish (*Zeugopterus punctatus*) start life as 'normal' two-sided fish. As they grow, one eye gradually migrates to join the other on one side, and they then take up life on the seabed. Pendennis Point, Falmouth. Nikon D100, Light and Motion housing, 105 mm macro, Inon Quad flash gun, ISO 200 f11 1/125.

PAGE 66: Dover sole (*Solea solea*) is a valuable commercial species, and is not often seen underwater. Once found, they are convinced that their camouflage protects them and will allow a very close approach. Roskilly's Cove, Newlyn, Mount's Bay. Nikon D200, Subal housing, 12–24 mm zoom, Subtronic Mini flash guns, ISO 100 f11 1/60.

PAGE 66 (bottom): Thornback rays (*Raja clavata*) are very much at home on sand and gravel seabeds, with which their colour, pattern and body shape blend almost perfectly. Yet they are quite nervous, and often swim away when approached. Porthcurno Bay. Nikon D200, Subal housing, 12–24 mm zoom, Subtronic Mini flash guns, ISO 100 f8 1/30.

PAGE 67: Thornback rays (*Raja clavata*) are most often seen on sandy seabeds, but occasionally they venture inshore to explore a reef for prey. Pendennis Point, Falmouth. Nikon F90X, Subal housing, 18–35 mm zoom, YS120 and YS30 flash guns, Fujichrome Velvia 50 ASA, f8 1/60.

PAGE 67 (bottom): Thornback rays (*Raja clavata*) belong to the shark family, but unlike many sharks do not bear live young. They lay their eggs in a 'mermaid's purse' (as do dogfish) which is often to be found attached to kelp stypes in shallow water. Pendennis Point, Falmouth. Nikon D100, Light and Motion housing, 12–24 mm zoom, Subtronic Mini flash guns, ISO 200 f8 1/30.

PAGE 68: Pollack (*Pollachius pollachius*) are commonly encountered around inshore and offshore reefs where they hunt smaller species, often working in packs to corner their prey. Minack Reef, Porthcurno Bay. Nikon D200, Subal housing, 12–24 mm zoom, Subtronic Mini flash guns, ISO 100 f8 1/30.

PAGE 69: Pouting or bib (*Trisopterus luscus*) are often known as wreck fish, as they seem to like the dark overhangs and protection that wrecks provide. Low Lee Reef, Mount's Bay. Nikon D200, Subal housing, 12–24 mm zoom, Subtronic Mini flash guns, ISO 100 f8 1/30.

PAGE 69: Pouting or bib (*Trisopterus luscus*) can be found schooling together, often in large shoals of several hundred fish. They show little fear of divers and can be approached easily. Low Lee Reef, Mount's Bay. Nikon D200, Subal housing, 12–24mm zoom, Subtronic Mini flash guns, ISO 100 f8 1/30.

PAGE 70: The basking shark (*Cetorhinus maximus*) is the second largest fish in the ocean (only the whale shark is bigger), reaching lengths of 10 m (33 ft). It is often mistaken for more dangerous species. Mount's Bay. Nikon D200, Subal housing, 12–24 mm zoom, ISO 200 f8 1/30.

PAGE 70: Basking sharks (*Cetorhinus maximus*) begin to appear in late spring and early summer with the first plankton blooms. They are totally harmless to snorkellers and will ignore a close approach while feeding. During some summers they are often only a few metres from popular beaches, and it is an unforgettable experience to swim close to this large fish. Mount's Bay. Nikon D200, Subal housing, 12–24 mm zoom, ISO 200 f8 1/30.

PAGE 71: Although the basking shark (*Cetorhinus maximus*) looks quite fearsome, it is a harmless plankton-feeder which sifts nutrients from large amounts of seawater as it swims along with its huge mouth wide open. Mount's Bay. Nikon D200, Subal housing, 12–24 mm zoom, ISO 200 f8 1/30.

PAGE 72: Compass jellyfish (*Chrysaora hysoscella*) arrive with the first plankton bloom of summer, and are sometimes seen in large numbers close to beaches. They have a mild sting, so should be avoided by swimmers. Pendennis Point, Falmouth. Nikon D100, Light and Motion housing, 18-35mm zoom, Subtronic Mini flash guns, ISO 200 f11 1/30.

PAGE 73: Rhizostoma jellyfish (*Rhizostoma octopus*) is sometimes called the 'dustbin lid' or 'barrel' jellyfish due to its size, which reaches almost a metre (3 ft) in diameter. During some summers there are hundreds of these jellyfish in certain areas, but their sting is harmless to humans. Porthkerris Cove, Lizard. Nikon F90X, Subal housing, 16 mm fisheye, YS120 and YS30 flash guns, Fujichrome Velvia 50 ASA, f16 1/60.

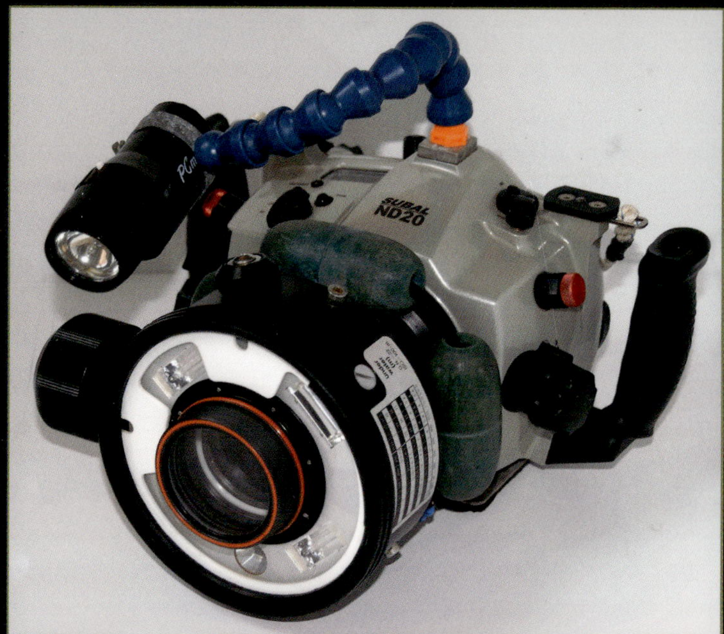

Nikon D200 in a Subal waterproof housing fitted with an Inon Quad flash (ring flash) for macro photography.

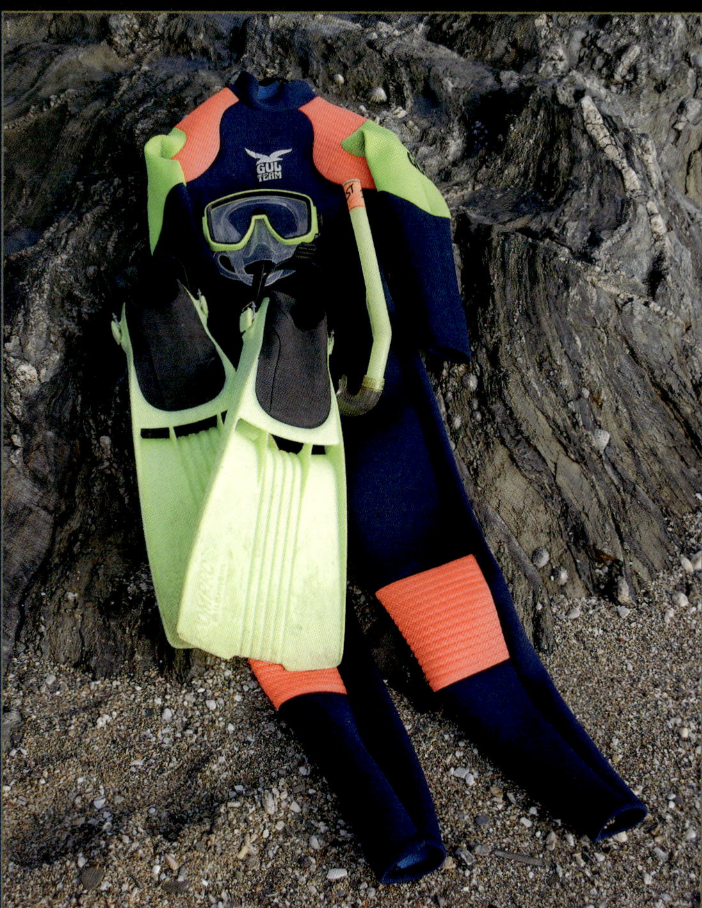

Simple snorkelling equipment is all you need for exploring the shallow waters of Cornwall's coastline. A light wetsuit will keep

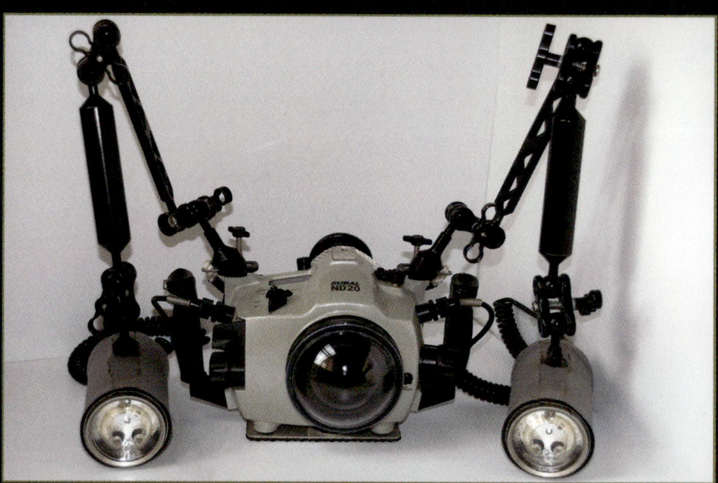

Nikon D200 in a Subal waterproof housing fitted with a fisheye lens and dome port for wide-angle photography. Two wide-angle